[handwritten inscription] Blessings on Bill ... Thank you for all you do to make "a place of God" all our lives

Life's Transitions:

Invitations to Wholeness

[handwritten inscription, left margin] Blessings to my friend Bill Ben Johnson 1-24-16

[handwritten inscription, bottom] My dear friend Bill... I'm filled with gratitude for our shared journey and the love that binds us together. You are a light!! With joy, Kay

Life's Transitions:

Invitations to Wholeness

by
Robby Carroll
Ben Johnson
Kay Stewart

Pathways Press
Atlanta, GA

ISBN 978-1518691836

Copies of this book may be ordered from:

www.Amazon.com

or

Pathways Press
PO Box 98213
Atlanta GA 30359

Contents

Contents

PART I

INTRODUCTION

PREFACE

Have patience with everything unresolved in your heart and try to love the questions themselves as if they were locked rooms or books written in a very foreign language. Don't search for the answers, which could not be given to you now because you would not be able to live them. And, the point is to live everything. Live the questions now. Perhaps then, someday far in the future, you will gradually, without even noticing it, live your way into the answer.

-Rainer Maria Rilke's Letters to a Young Poet (1934)

An invitation

This book is about life's transitions – it's an invitation to *live the questions* of a life in transition, and to *live them now!* This is not a book of theories, concepts, strategies, or advice. Rather, it is a collection of real stories coupled with an invitation to connect occurrences to resources deep within us. The book is also about letting go of our striving for answers . . . it's an invitation simply to *live* the stories and questions, and perhaps gradually live into a sense of wholeness through lessons learned! We encourage you to engage the book with openness and curiosity, bringing patience and gentleness to all it stirs in you.

These pages reflect the light and life discovered in real people, real sharing, and real stories. The writing of this book came through a series of conversations among your authors. For more than a year they met to candidly share their own stories of healing, growth, and wholeness. Together they lived the questions of their transitions. Connections were strengthened by listening deeply and reflecting on unique stories that revealed subtle, yet powerful common threads of their human experience. By engaging these stories, their hearts were opened, their souls were stirred, and they were enabled to more fully live the transitions of their lives.

The authors – Kay Stewart, Robby Carroll and Ben Johnson – are story-gatherers and inquiry partners. Together, they represent more than two hundred years of living. Collectively, they have lived through tragic loss, challenging opportunities, fearful hours of darkness, and countless other experiences that created transitions for them. They did not always make those transitions successfully. Sometimes they got stuck in a transition, other times they were overwhelmed, and often they were surprised by the blessings called forth through their transitions.

Meet the authors

Kay teaches mindfulness and leads workshops and retreats to help participants cultivate a way of being in the world that is large enough to hold mind, body, heart, and spirit. Her passion for health and well-being emerged through the loss of both her parents and her only brother early in life. Her teaching encourages mindful living, joyful connection, and wise action. Kay bubbles with enthusiasm as she invites us to slow down, focus, and pay attention to what matters most in our work, our relationships, and our health.

For more than thirty years, Robby has been a counselor and a pastor. After overcoming his own addiction, he has walked with many who are conquering theirs. His insights, compassion, and broad perspective have been highly effective in helping others find their way through some of life's most challenging transitions. Robby exudes kindness and warmth, and he embodies unbridled joy and a contagious zest for wholehearted living.

Ben has been a pastor, an entrepreneur, a professor and a business consultant. He has transitioned from having no faith to finding and growing spiritually in a personal faith. He inspires growth and connection, and he is always seeking new ways to grow as he shares lessons learned through his knowledge and experience. Ben has a gift for seeing and calling forth the wisdom inside us all. Having lived more than eight decades through insights, trial and error, and numerous failings, he has found his way to a meaningful, joyous life.

In reading the stories on the pages that follow, we hope you discover something that informs and shapes your life. Read expectantly, the stories will evoke questions for reflection that may illuminate life-giving possibilities amidst the inevitable changes, alterations and shifts in your relationships.

With reverence and gratitude for all that is represented in our individual and collective stories, we invite you to open your heart and listen for the stories that are called up in you. As you live the questions that these stories call forth, perhaps you will see yourself more clearly and discover the wholeness awaiting you. As you make this journey, we hope you will receive enough light to illuminate the next step in your life's ever-changing adventure. As we all continue to live the transitions of our lives, we will discover that life's most important lessons open us to fulfillment and wholeness.

How to read this book

Whether you choose to engage one story, just a few, or all of them, simply be open to the essence of each story in a gentle, unhurried way. It isn't necessary to read the stories in order, though they roughly follow in chronological order from youth through old age. Notice which stories draw you in and listen generously to what stirs or touches you, living the questions that arise in the stories you choose to engage.

Let these stories and the questions they inspire be a reminder that ALL of life is really transition. Life is not a goal to be attained; it is an unfolding mystery to be experienced. The more we experience real life (that's code for getting older!), the more we know this to be true.

May the stories that follow illuminate life's transitions as invitations to wholeness.

PART II

STORIES OF TRANSITIONS

1. A Teenage Search for Identity

"Reading gives me a backboard to bounce my ideas off, and in reading I discover something of who I am and what is important to me."

I felt both honored and challenged when I was asked to write my story. As a teenager, I was honored to think that my story might mean something to other people; I was challenged to discover myself and to relate it to others. Here's hoping that what I write will help other teenagers discover themselves and other parents learn to relate to their teenagers.

In my lifetime, my family has lived in two states and five cities. As the firstborn in our family of four, my being an "only child" was short-lived. My only brother was born eleven months after me, so for a brief time each year, we're the same age! We've now lived in our current home for nine years, the longest we've lived in one place. These numbers point toward lots of transitions, and I realize that maturing through the many transitions of life is partly about age, yet growing up requires looking at much more than numbers.

When I think about the transition into my teen years, the first thing that comes to my mind is a huge maturity difference. Many of the things that seemed so important to who I was at twelve are just not that significant at sixteen. When I was twelve, the boy – girl relationship felt like such a huge deal. A breakup felt like the end of the world, especially since I was the one being left. Playing boyfriend/girlfriend was the biggest drama on the playground.

During my years in middle elementary school, I began to feel an interest in the opposite sex and had an urge to make a connection with a boy. Today it feels like those experiences and emotions are worlds away, and you might be surprised to hear these relationships have stopped being so central to my social life. In middle school, if a friend had a crush on a boy I liked, it could cause a huge drama. I don't see that as much today, and as high-schoolers we have moved past that slightly. Most of us are too worried about our futures, colleges, etc., to be so deeply concerned with a relationship, though I cannot speak for all teenagers. And that's not to say that teenage relationships don't feel important – they do, but there are other ways to relate to your friends than just whom you're attracted to. When we have a breakup, we hopefully put it in perspective and realize how much else there is to life besides whether or not we are single.

Computers and Social Media

As I reflect on the difference between twelve and sixteen, I see not only a change in my emotional maturity and feelings, but also sense that I live in a different world from the one that my mom and dad knew when they were my age. Today at sixteen my connections are not made on the playground, but out in the cyberworld. Instead of playing tag on the playground, we play tag on the Internet. For example, someone in the school lunchroom will schedule a time for everyone to log on to their laptops. We all meet in the Gmail Chat Room where we have a group chat together; in this social encounter a lot of relationships begin and end.

Sometimes there are serious conflicts in these chat rooms. An incident comes to mind that happened over Gmail when I was about thirteen. At the time, Facebook was not available. In our chat room conversation, someone spoke rudely about my brother. I retaliated in kind, and pretty soon it turned into a war between my friends and people who attended school with my brother. We were having a fierce war online just because someone said something abusive about my brother. I got defensive and they got defensive, resulting in an explosive torrent of words and feelings.

Beyond the emotional explosions and conflicts, social media of today also help us keep up with people, especially those who are important friends. Twitter and Instagram provide connections for scores of teenagers. I think Facebook has taken a backseat in the social networking experience for people my age; it's mostly used by people who don't have other social media sites, though it does offer a medium convenient for communicating with adults. For example, if I want to communicate with an adult like my pastor or my choir leader, I use Facebook.

Facebook itself is in transition, as I see younger people using it in a different way. In most of my classes there are groups meeting on Facebook. For example, there is a group for my Advanced Placement (AP) world history class. If I have a question about a world history assignment, I can post it on the Facebook group page, and all thirty people in the class can see my request for help and respond to it.

Social media also offer a significant change in how teens connect, organize, and experience parties. If there's a party, the group is invited through social media. When one person gets invited to the party, that individual may bring one or two friends, and her friends may bring their friends. Before long there is a really big party with a lot of surprise guests. Often there are numerous social gatherings in the homes of teenagers whose parents are not around. In this setting things can happen that are not very good, and these party participants create stereotypes that label them or get projected onto large groups of young people.

Teenagers find that Twitter provides a means of blowing off steam. Twitter has character limits; a message cannot go over a hundred words. So Twitter is created for short, brief, emotional explosions like the kind a person uses to take the pressure off one's mind. One day I felt irritated about my schedule and tweeted, "I'm so angry!" I probably tweeted those words five times or more. You see a great deal of this blowing off steam when people are deeply frustrated.

Social media definitely open up grounds for bullying, and while some of us have matured since middle school, there are a number who have not. "Subtweets" happen when you tweet about persons without tagging them in it – it's the Internet equivalent of talking about people behind their back. I've had things said about me, and it can be painful to see people "like" hurtful things. These exchanges have sparked many anti-cyber bullying campaigns and even laws, but most teens (typically the ones who do the bullying) just laugh at them. Because they sit anonymously behind a keyboard, they feel untouchable.

Struggles Today

Though social media bring unique challenges, the greatest pressure I experience as a sixteen-year-old sophomore in high school is preparing for college. I work very hard to keep my grades up and carry a high GPA. In my school this diligent work is necessary because all the students must maintain a certain GPA to remain in the school. Because of this demand, I feel lots of pressure to study hard and make good grades so that I will be able to get into a good college. Since my school is so competitive, I am driven to be the best that I can be. I feel pressure daily as I strive to get the highest test score in order to get into the best college. Pressure is intensified by teachers telling us their class takes priority over all the others. From the drama coach claiming that play rehearsals take priority to coaches of various sports teams claiming that every practice and game takes priority, it feels overwhelming. When I have all these people telling me what should be my priority, it's really easy to lose sight of what I personally value and see as a priority. Often my judgment is that the bar has been set so high that it is unattainable.

On the other hand, there are students in my school who really don't care about their grades; their biggest issue is what party or concert to attend and with whom. I feel somewhat conflicted when I see pictures of my classmates on social media attending a concert. One night a number of friends were chatting on the Internet about having gone to a particular performance, and I wondered how they had the time to attend on a school night. I suppose that it depends on what one's goals are for their life or how seriously they take their future.

A person might wonder if this intense competition leads to cutthroat behavior in the school. Interestingly, in some ways competition actually brings us closer together. Even if we are at each other's throats about turning in the best paper or getting a certain solo or landing the lead role in a play, we all know what it feels like to lose out. Instead of gloating, those who win are generally sympathetic and supportive toward those who lost. For example, I have an understudy in one of the musicals, and she had really wanted to get the lead role. We are good friends and she was very gracious about my getting the lead role; she has given me her complete support. So the competition is not as cutthroat as one might think. All of us understand that everyone cannot be the lead in every play or in every musical; and since we all know how it feels not to be chosen, we have good reasons to be understanding and compassionate to one another.

Living with Uncertainty and "Pressure-Packed Schedules"

When I think about my future, without a doubt college is the biggest thing on my mind. Am I going to get into my dream school? I'm always checking myself to discern if I am lowering my standards or taking the easy route. Sometimes I find myself wondering if I can get into the school of my choice. After all, it is difficult to get into a school that accepts only ten or twelve percent of thousands of applicants. When I feel this stress, I wonder what I should do. Do I lower my expectations? I feel a little bit frightened because I wonder what the world will be like when I'm thirty. Sometimes, the future does not look bright to me. When I look back from age thirty, how will I evaluate some of the decisions that I am making today? I really don't want to let my parents down, nor do I want to let myself down.

I know I have the potential to do something great with my life, but at sixteen it feels so difficult. My classmates struggle, too, and many of my friends go home from school and have breakdowns at the end of the day. I think the stress factor has really changed since my teachers or my parents were in school; my social studies teacher told her class that if she were a sixteen-year-old and in my school today, she would not take an AP class next year. I am taking three AP classes and still doing all the things I'm engaged in, and this brings a lot of pressure. One thing that can be said about teenagers today is "their schedule is pressure-packed."

Sometimes I ask myself, "Am I working hard at school to get approval from my parents and teachers? Am I so deeply engaged because I want to make my life a success?" In this struggle I keep reminding myself that I am a human being and I have to decide how much stress and pressure I can handle. Should I not be willing to give up some opportunities so that I don't lose my mind?

As I reflect on these questions, my decision about involvement in tour groups at my school comes to mind. Tour groups would be equivalent to a varsity sports team in other schools. This year I was in the drama tour group, which is an exclusive, elite, acting troupe. I also got into the elite show choir group, an amazing experience which I loved. I learned so much, but it required rehearsal every day from four o'clock until seven o'clock for six out of the nine months of the school year. With this demand, I was incredibly stressed. I know that next year I will be taking three AP classes, but I really wanted to stay in the drama ensemble too.

Recently, I talked to the directors of both groups and to the person in charge of scheduling. I decided to go with the show choir even though this would mean not being in the exclusive drama group which would have offered me numerous opportunities to be a leader. I truly want to learn how to be a leader, but I must be honest with myself about the amount of stress that I can handle.

Vision for the future

Today I have a vision for my life when I am grown. When I am thirty years old, I would love to have a house in North Carolina. By that time I expect to be married and probably have two kids. I dream of having a successful career. At this point in my life I think that I'm going to get a law degree and practice law or enter into politics. I want to establish myself in the practice of law, take hard cases, and set new precedents for creating a more just society. Before I die, I want to have an impact on our society. I want to change the way that people look at women's roles in society along with the attitudes that many have of minorities and their roles in society. I want to do something that will create equal opportunity for everyone who loves this country. So when I come to the end of my career, I want to know I've made a difference in the world.

Getting to Know Myself

A lot of what I think of myself comes from what I hear from other teenagers, my peers. When someone expresses an opinion that I really agree with or one I really don't agree with, I make a judgment for myself. So what I think and believe is a response to what I hear others saying; it helps me to sharpen my point of view. We are social creatures and for me it means to be an extrovert; just hearing what other people say and sensing my reactions to them tells me something about who I am. This experience helps me discover what is important to me or what I think is right or what I think demands priority. It also helps me discover what I believe and what I want to do, and what I want to accomplish.

I also think that reading is important; books can provide a mirror in which to view yourself. When I read a book, it can change the way I think. Sometimes when I am reading, I begin to filter my thoughts through the author's voice. When I read, ideas occur to me that I hadn't thought of or even if I had thought along those lines, I did not know how to articulate my thoughts. Reading gives me a backboard to bounce my ideas off, and in reading I discover something of who I am and what is important to me.

If someone were to persist in asking, "Who are you?" I would say that I am a feminist, a student, and a lover of equality and justice, and I love to perform. I'm a Christian, I am someone who cares deeply about the feelings and wellbeing of other people, I'm someone who loves to exercise, loves to dance, loves to sleep, loves to be around other people, loves to read, loves spending time with my cats and my parents, especially with my parents.

I am often extremely distressed; I worry 24/7 about the state of the world and wonder what the future will be and what our government will look like when I am grown. I wonder what difference I will make in the world when I can vote and begin taking decisive stands to bring about a change. Just saying these things underscores how very scary it is to think about the future. When I think about all the things happening in the world and my inability to do anything about it, I feel helpless and discouraged. So what am I to do? I feel like I cannot do anything now; I'm worried that even when I'm old enough to express an opinion about world issues, nobody will listen. I am anxious that I won't be able to do anything to right the wrongs in the world.

Sex and Drugs in High School

At an arts school we get a disproportionate share of those people who feel themselves to be enlightened. Many of them at my school smoke marijuana and tobacco. I fear that I have lost two friends who now seem quite distant because of these habits. I have lost them because they are spending their weekends drinking and doing drugs, which causes them to do dangerous things. Many of these friends of mine are miserable and try to solve their frustration and fear with alcohol and drugs. This choice inevitably makes their boredom and frustration worse; they are on a downward spiral which is perpetuating the cycle. I have tried to speak to them, but they won't listen to me. I suppose that I have lost many of my friends because we don't have much in common. Realizing the change I have made makes me want to shout, "Yeah. Yeah. Yeah."

One of my longtime friends comes to mind. We used to be inseparable and then he began making decisions I didn't agree with – they were dangerous to his health and damaging to his self-respect, and I know that his low self-esteem is a result. But some of the things he's doing today are only making his life worse. For many teens the ideal weekend or spring break is going to the beach and drinking 24/7, and smoking like a fiend. This kind of behavior is glorified like the Holy Grail of Spring Breaks.

This same male friend got drunk one night and had sex with a girl who is a good friend of mine. That was the last straw with me. I think that his choices are detrimental to his mental state as well as damaging the girl's reputation and her self-respect. The stigma that sex is bad or evil should not be imposed on us. However, it takes a lot of maturity to engage in such an intimate relationship, and I think we have to accept ourselves completely before we can ever involve ourselves in this intimacy. If you aren't happy with yourself when you are by yourself, you can't be happy with someone else.

I think one problem among teenagers today stems from people who feel that they are broken, and they try to fix their brokenness by using someone else who is broken. This situation ends up as a toxic, unhealthy relationship. When sex is brought into the equation, the ground of the relationship is dreadfully shaky.

Sources of Strength

My greatest source of strength is my mom, which is a unique attitude among many of my friends. Some would say that most teenagers don't have healthy relationships with their parents or at least they feel distant, but I can honestly say that my mom is my best friend. When I have a really terrible day and come home stressed out, for a few minutes I unload on her. I know that I can say anything and she will support me and help me through whatever I am facing.

In addition to having an understanding mom, I get strength from doing one thing that is just purely self-indulgent, like finding one moment throughout the day when I stop thinking about everything else and relax. In that quiet space I take a moment to focus on my immediate needs. I take time to give myself a little self-love because that's important too. At the end of the day, I sometimes set aside thirty minutes to take a nice, long bath. At other times I take a thirty-minute nap or go outside to just be in nature. I love the outdoors, so spending time outside and getting away from all the little petty things seems really important. There is something relaxing about turning off the phone and getting back to my roots. Many of us spend so much time inside a building, be it at home or at school, that we forget how important and healing nature can be.

Build a Trusting Relationship

My warm and open relationship with my mom came after about two years of reporting my whereabouts dishonestly, lying about what I was doing and sneaking around and taking part in some of the forbidden activities with my friends. I took this path of deception after I came to my new school. I made new friends, a lot of whom had parents who didn't really care what they did. It became really easy for me to go over to their house where we had free reign without any supervision. I made some poor decisions that I wish I'd never made. I lied to my parents about where I was and what I was doing.

Eventually they found out about my deceit on a couple of occasions last year. After I was caught, I decided to confess completely, but then I reverted back to old behaviors until this year, when I chose to become honest about a relationship. Even though my parents disapproved, I came clean about it; I came clean about literally everything else that I had ever done. Most of these things they didn't know about. As a consequence of my slipping around, I was completely grounded for the whole semester. I had no phone, no going anywhere on the weekends, and no computer time except for school work. With these restraints in place, we started talking about everything. In a strange way when I became completely honest about where I was going and what I was doing, I actually began experiencing more freedom.

My parents helped me to see that if they knew where I was and what I was doing, even if they didn't approve, at least they had the information. If necessary, they knew how to find me and pick me up if I needed their help. This relationship with my parents is so different from many of my friends. A large number of my friends have parents with no idea what they're doing on the weekends. They could be in imminent danger and no one would know where to look for them.

When I told my parents everything, at first they were horrified. One of the hardest things for me was the shame that I felt; it was so difficult for me to recall my actions and to get the words out of my mouth. I was terrified about the punishment that I might receive. I figured that I would be unable do anything for the rest of the time I lived at home. Perhaps when I was eighteen and out of the house, I could end my house arrest. Teenagers don't realize what could help them; we think that the worst our parents can do is to take away our privileges for six months. What we do not realize is how much this discipline can help us get a grip on our lives. I am grateful for parents who care where I am and what I am doing! When I was engaged in my undisciplined behavior, if anyone had asked me if I would trade that deceptive life for an honest relationship with my parents, my answer would have been a no-brainer! Foolishly, I would have chosen to keep partying on the weekends. But the honest relationship that I now have with my parents is such a source of joy in my life that I would not trade it for anything, even all the weekend parties in town.

My answer might sound very lame to another sixteen-year-old, but the one thing that makes me most happy is that I can tell my mom anything! Now I have more freedom and no guilt about my life. My parents want me to be safe and if something goes wrong, I can talk with them about it. They trust me, and the last thing I want to do is lose that trust. I think probably the best advice that I could give other teens is to be honest with their parents.

Life is so much better since I have been honest with my parents, and we have developed a more loving and trusting relationship. I feel sad when I look at some of the relationships that my friends have with their parents; things are really confused with many of them. I know that parents are different; it appears to me that some parents prefer not to know what their kids are doing. It has never been that way for me because my parents aren't like that. The mom of a good friend has taken the "don't ask, don't tell" approach. Her mom said quite candidly, "I do not want to know what you're doing." Hearing her relate this made me sad. Even though we think that adults don't understand, even though we rebel and say that we don't need adults, we really do.

About My Faith

My story might become clearer with a little background on my faith journey. We went to church when we lived in Carrollton, Georgia; I was young and church did not mean much to me. When we lived in Virginia, we were very involved in church. When we moved to Atlanta, we didn't find one that fit us, and our lives seemed too busy for church anyway. Then we joined Shallowford Presbyterian Church about two years ago. Until then, religion and faith had not been big on my radar screen.

Actually, a number of things scared me away from Christianity. I had seen so many people in churches who were narrow-minded and who judged others harshly, that I didn't care to be involved with a church. When I came to the church that I now attend, I realized that being a Christian is living what you read in the parables – Jesus was loving and compassionate; everyone mattered to him. He especially cared for the social outcasts. I think that if Jesus were on earth today, he would love you no matter what your sexual orientation is, what your gender is, what you look like or what you believe in. I think that God loves everyone, and being reminded of that seems to be enough.

When I think about my sources of strength and joy, I believe that God is my greatest source. My relation to God is somewhat like my relationship with my parents, except God is greater than we can comprehend. Just like I can tell my mom anything, I can talk to God about anything. That's just amazing to me, and it makes me feel really close to God.

Last summer I went on the choir tour; I went to Montreat, our denomination's retreat center, and I also took part in a mission trip. On the mission trip, each morning we had brief devotionals. We were given journals to write reflections on our relationship with God. We also prayed and dedicated our time to God and went out to serve people. It was an amazing experience. I think that serving others and realizing that I'm doing it for God makes me feel good. I think that serving others starts with just talking to somebody, like going up to someone and saying "Hi." We also have a duty to serve people who

aren't as fortunate as we are. I think that's what I'm most proud of –
being a Christian. When I am connecting and doing these things for
others, I really feel closest to God.

2. Scars of Teenage Punishment

*"By tapping into that deeply rooted sense of belonging
and joy that was seeded by my grandmother, I am
able to flow through good times and bad, discovering
healing and peace in the streams of influence that
open me to love and be loved."*

Vivid memories stir in me around one particular school day when I was in the seventh grade. I can almost hear the sound of the ringing phone that evening, and feel my heart pounding when I realized it was my teacher. She asked to speak with my father, and I could sense his building anger as the conversation progressed. When my father got off the phone, he was filled with rage. Even now I can feel his rage penetrate me as he entered my room shouting, "So what is this about you telling dirty jokes to girls in your class? Tell me those jokes you thought were so funny. TELL ME!! Tell me now!!" With fear coursing through me, I pleaded with him saying that I had not been telling dirty jokes. It soon became clear to me that my father's mind was made up about me, and he was not willing to listen. Sadly, I decided the only way I could end the conversation and move from this painful moment was to make up a joke and accept his shame and punishment.

This experience convinced me that my father did not really care for me, that it did not matter to him whether I succeeded or failed. The only thing he seemed willing to accept was his perception of what I had done. What mattered most to my father was that the teacher calling about my behavior was embarrassing to him. Whether I had told girls jokes or not, the fact that the teacher called about his son angered him. He was not interested in exploring the truth from my view or considering further the perception of me in the mind of the teacher.

The very next year my father sent me away from home to an all-boys school. I had deep feelings of sadness, loss, and grief, and I feared being alone. Scarred by my father's rage, I made the determination that no one really cared about my feelings of isolation. I was unable to express or talk about feelings, and no one seemed willing to listen to me. I did not feel heard and accepted. I vividly recall the day that my mother and father took me to the school and dumped me and my luggage there for a year. I remember feeling all alone and desperately wanting to hide. I soon found a large growth of bushes on the athletic field, and I sat there behind them, hiding from school authorities and other students on my first day, just crying and crying for what seemed like a very long time.

From the moment I arrived, I felt homesick, frightened and alone. To be misunderstood, jerked out of my family setting, and sent off to school was not only disrupting but exceedingly frightening. I felt like I was a captive in a foreign land.

Feelings of isolation and fear were heightened when the school registrar determined that I had to repeat the seventh grade. This meant that I was placed with the youngest boys in the school, and we endured hazing on a daily basis by the upperclassmen. We simply had to take what the older ones dished out to us.

Being away from home and from the biggest source of security in my life, my grandmother, felt overwhelming. This sense of being alone, coupled with being forced to face abuse by the faculty and older students, increased the pain and isolation in my life in significant ways. Yet, these experiences also strengthened me by making it clear to me that I was totally on my own, responsible for myself. This awareness forced me to develop my inner resources to deal with the alienation and the absence of warmth and caring that I craved. Looking backward at this experience, I recognize that the things that happened to me in boarding school laid the groundwork for life transitions that were yet to come.

The feelings of helplessness and isolation in one sense are still alive in me. Though I have overcome most of the despair associated with early painful experiences, those same feelings have become energized and transformed in healing ways through similar events. When my son struggled with learning disabilities, mental illness, and addiction, I worked diligently to be with him in his frustration and despair. My capacity to be with him was fueled by feelings that I had experienced when I was sent away.

I'm also aware that feelings of isolation and sadness have played a significant role in my work as a therapist. Though I now have a sense of peace and a quick recognition of those old feelings, this does not keep them from arising in my consciousness. I will never forget what it felt like to be alone and without relational emotional resources.

Both before and after going away to boarding school, when I was home with my parents I was caught up in their conflict. Through my pain and alienation at school, I decided to face my parents with the tough skin I had developed with the students at school, yet the urge to run away was still alive in me. My connection with my grandmother was also alive in me, stirring feelings of acceptance and warmth. When I was with my grandmother, I always felt safe, cared for, and unconditionally loved.

Fully accepting care from others continues to be an area of growth for me. A fear of becoming dependent lingers in me, even as I'm aware of my desire to discover new ways to let the love and good will of people flow more completely into my life. Yet, I still know that taking responsibility for my life and what I do with it is important, and I generally work to keep my options open so that I have pathways of escape if they are needed. The most important lesson that I learned at boarding school is that I can land on my feet and that I can survive in challenging and difficult situations.

I have been able to look for the opportunities to grow and change through each crisis that I face in life. In times of pain, loss, and disappointment, I have developed the capacity to lean into suffering and find my way through.

Grief and pain are very alive in me as I write this, because I am conscious of great fear and despair over my dear son. I love him so deeply, and not knowing where he is right now is almost too excruciating to face. One of the ways I'm dealing with his disappearance is to work even more intensely and harder than normal. With him missing, I find that I am up at three o'clock in the morning, not simply staring at the walls, but reading or writing or organizing so that I am somehow using my grief and depression in productive and redemptive ways.

Is substituting work for worry necessarily running away or avoidance? I'm responding to my loss of contact with my son by using my work as a way to move through pain, uncertainty, and loss. I'm aware that my personality is described as an adventurer based on the assessment of a well-known self-awareness tool called the Enneagram. The adventurer tends to run towards adventure, new things, and new insights. The adventurer tends to run away from pain even as he is saying "yes" to be productive. My chosen response may be avoidance and if it is, I see it as something over which I have little control. At those moments when life seems more than I can bear, I usually get into bed, pull the covers up over my head, and seek total darkness. Sometimes I essentially check out when the conflict within becomes more than I can handle, seeking a way to survive when I feel off balance.

My experiences and feelings from early adolescence are perhaps, in many ways, no different from what all young people face when they are uncertain about who they are. Those feelings of isolation and the ways I learned to cope have found expression again and again at later points in my life. On one level I can still turn inward and, in a sense, find that safe hiding place, walking away if necessary. At the same time, I can be transparent and wide open to the love that surrounds me. By tapping into that deeply rooted sense of belonging and joy that was seeded by my grandmother, I am able to flow through good times and bad, discovering healing and peace in the streams of influence that open me to love and be loved.

3. A Young Person's Awakening

"Maybe, I thought, the simple act of listening for once constituted prayer."

The following story comes in the form of an essay written by a minister's son who had given his father every indication that he was agnostic with respect to God. Because he had accepted a call to a new church that took him away from home, the father was removed from monitoring the daily actions of his son, a high school senior. The young man was living with his grandparents, who welcomed the opportunity to shepherd him through his last year of high school. Out of the blue the father received a letter from his son that contained an essay written to gain admission to a prominent university in his home state. In the letter he said, "The topic and the content of the essay were surprises to me!"

The Essay

Fast-paced, energetic music accompanied my brisk walk down the carpet to my father's office. I swung the door open, tossed my backpack into the nearest chair, and took off the headphones. "Dad, I'm done with my work. When can we leave?" My father looked up slowly from the tome covering his desk. "In about half an hour, Benjamin; you'll just have to be patient." With a discontented sigh, I turned abruptly. Wandering aimlessly outside, I puzzled over what I could possibly find entertaining inside my dad's church. Eventually arriving at the sanctuary, and having run out of power in my phone, I pulled open the heavy doors.

The cavernous expanse that awaited me was silent, save for the constant pouring of water in the baptismal font. It was bizarre seeing the massive room so empty; on most Sunday mornings it was teeming with life. As I paced alongside the rows of pews, I became increasingly aware of the disruption my footsteps were causing on the otherwise calm atmosphere; instinctively I slowed down. Growing more tranquil, I closed my eyes and gradually tuned in to the sound of my heart, a rhythmic

31

beating that was solitary in its song, a lone drummer releasing successive, smooth waves that reverberated through me. The drummer had always been with me, of course, but I had long since become deaf to him, his soft vibrations often lost among the competing sounds of life.

As I sank further into reverie, I slowly became aware of a change in light; I opened my eyes to see the sun shining through the circular stained glass window. I stood up and started towards the altar. Radiant beams fell upon me as I drew closer, bathing my skin and clothes in a faint veil of energy. I slowly shifted my face up towards the centerpiece of the crystalline window, basking in the warmth of its touch. It felt transcendent, as though in some small way, a piece of something divine or cosmic was currently in transit, and I alone was its witness. In just a few minutes I had been completely stripped of my life's incessant white noise that for so long had dominated my consciousness. In its place came a serenity and sense of profundity. I walked to the font and felt compelled to dip my fingers into the coursing water that endlessly spilled over the transparent bowl. As the cool water trickled down my fingers, I contemplated what it meant to "pray."

For years I had known that on Sundays my father would go to church around dawn and pray for hours, but I had never understood why. Prayer had always been the mundane task of closing my eyes and clasping my hands until told to stop – a routine and meaningless gesture. Why then had these twenty minutes felt so different? Maybe, I thought, the simple act of listening for once constituted prayer. Maybe I had achieved this peace by stopping to appreciate the beauty of life in and of itself, unadulterated by a world constantly preoccupied with superficial concerns. Maybe life would become more meaningful if I would stop taking it for granted and start allowing for opportunities to be humbled by the miracle that is existence. By now my hand was submerged in the running water, and pulling it out created a downpour of droplets. Gazing deeply into the currents of water, I was interrupted by the abrupt sound of a door closing. My father's firm hand fell on my shoulder. "All right, we're good to go. I assume you're more than ready?" I nodded silently, and slowly turned to follow him out.

4. A Spiritual Collapse

"New life is given us, not to grasp but to receive and then to let it pass through us. Such can be if we learn to live in this moment and then the next and the next . . . "

Many sincere people begin a new phase of their life with strong intentions and high hopes. Some of these enthusiastic individuals get trapped in a way of life that ceases to be liberating and redemptive. The glorious and long-lasting results that were promised by teachers, models or spiritual leaders fail. I was one of those people, and I want to share my experience of living in darkness and finding that my map of life did not describe the territory over which I was passing. My experience was so conflicted and confused that I have spent nearly a lifetime trying to understand it.

At seventeen years old, I had a dramatic religious experience. Following this moment of spiritual transformation, I experienced a unity of my personhood, a positive vision of life and a sense that I now had a reason for living. I anticipated that the rest of my life would be filled with this bliss and happiness. My mentors encouraged me to read books that would be helpful, especially the Bible. I embraced the notion that I had to nurture this new life if it was to last. Those around me encouraged me to make a total commitment of my life to God if I intended to be an all-out Christian. They also made very clear to me the standards of the life that I had embraced: they stressed what I was to believe, what I was to do and how I was to be faithful. Doing all these things was meant to give me assurance that I was an authentic Christian.

For that first year I experienced a transformed consciousness. God was with me; Christ was in me; I felt that I was being led by God's Spirit. My life overflowed with joy and happiness. I experienced a freedom from depression, doubt and darkness. I learned to deflect the threatening questions that sometimes burrowed furtively into my consciousness. I know now that these suppressed questions should have been faced, struggled with, and *lived*, but instead I avoided them. I sought to keep on the trail and to conform my life to the image of life derived from Jesus Christ.

Following that first year of bliss, I began to feel the force of questions that I had somehow avoided. Mr. Chappell, an automobile mechanic whose shop was near my home, belonged to a Pentecostal church. He began talking with me about the Spirit in his church and in his daily life. He began to share with me his experiences in the Holy Spirit that were open to everyone. My spiritual mentors had warned me that the pathway he was describing was radical, fanatical, and purely emotional. Hearing Mr. Chappell's witness disturbed me and raised doubts in my mind about the quality of my faith. Was he right? Was my relation to God shallow and juvenile?

A few months after that encounter, I was invited to an evening prayer meeting held in the home of a local school teacher. At this meeting an older woman who sat across the room from me began expressing the presence of the Spirit in a strange language that I did not understand. The leader of the evening asked me if I desired to have the Spirit work in my life in the way that this woman had demonstrated. I was resistant because I could not betray my mentors who had advised me against this brand of religion.

The third experience that precipitated my emotional 'breakdown' filled me with fear, cast me into darkness and left me full of doubt. It came to me while I was speaking at a Methodist church in Point Washington, Florida. In this little town where boats ferried cars across the bay my friend and I were working with the congregation for a full week. One day we visited in the home of a former member of the Methodist church where we were conducting special services, and this woman of about twenty years began to talk about her reasons for leaving. I remember clearly the crushing experience that I had that day. I was sitting on a kitchen stool listening to this young woman describe the experience of God that she had when she left the Methodist church and began attending an Assembly of God church. She explained that a person who received the Holy Spirit spoke in tongues, and speaking in tongues was clear evidence of the Spirit within. She then proceeded to tell how she had received the Holy Spirit in this manner.

While she was speaking, in that very moment terror went through me like a streak of lightning; the fright was like a wedge entering my head and splitting me wide open. I was terrified. My consciousness was like a tent flapping in the wind without any tent pegs to hold it down. My fragile faith was bending and under duress with nothing to grasp and hold on to. Nothing seemed settled; my joy had evaporated; the bliss I had tasted for a year suddenly turned sour. I had to appear only one more time and dreaded the thought of speaking to others when my own faith suddenly seemed so weak.

After the service that evening I got in the car and began my trip home. The next day, Saturday, I made an appointment with our family doctor. He had practiced medicine in my hometown for years and was a trusted soul. When I got to his office, he took my vital signs and listened to me. He said there was nothing wrong with me that he could detect.

After my visit with the doctor on Saturday, the next day I drove to a little church in Vernledge, Alabama. I preached my first sermon on Sunday evening and the second on Monday evening. During the day on Monday, I walked the highway praying and wondering what was wrong with me. The more I thought about my condition, the more discouragement filled my thinking; fear flooded my mind. I felt deeply alienated from myself and from God. Darkness flowed from an open pit in my own inner being. I was overcome by this deep, dark void inside me. I felt like I had blackout of the soul and that I was on the edge of a precipice about to fall into outer darkness. For me, this meant falling into nothingness. I was so distraught that I called a friend of mine and asked him to substitute for me in the church for the remainder of the week.

When I got home, I tried to tell my mother what was happening to me, but I had no words to express the experience that I did not understand. Later my mother confided to me that she thought I was having a nervous breakdown. This explosion of soul happened just before my departure for college. I had repressed and/or suppressed most of my fears and doubts.

When I got to college, I sought to show my classmates a fellow who was joyous and happy. I presented myself as a dedicated servant of God (this is what I hoped I would be, yet I was fighting a fierce

35

battle on the inside). I had many opportunities to travel throughout the state preaching in all kinds of churches and youth gatherings. I had opportunities to speak to numerous groups, but especially youth. Even though I appeared to be on top of my game, often when I spoke to others, the frightening voice inside said to me, "You are a sinner and in greater need than these people sitting in front of you. You are going to hell because you have committed the unpardonable sin."

During a chapel service in which students were giving witness to their faith, I recall standing before the student body and saying, "Pray for me; I fear that I have committed the unpardonable sin." Nobody spoke to me after that confession; no one seemed to take me seriously. Perhaps they thought it was all part of an act, but it was not; it was a cry of desperation. In this Christian college I was sending signals of deep distress, but nobody ever talked with me or explored with me what was going on in my soul. I was suffering silently while feeling hypocritical, divided and alone.

During this dark period, one saving thing occurred in my life; I met a fellow student who had had a similar experience. Through our mutual sharing, I began to get a modicum of relief. As I began to get my bearing, I was like a drowning man; I had washed up on the sandy beach of a distant island and was clawing my way up the beach in search of safety on dry land.

How do I understand this overwhelming experience six decades later? First of all, this experience and the time of testing came to me at a very vulnerable age. I was seventeen without a strong sense of self, with lots of fear in my mind that was generated by a hellfire and damnation revival preacher. His preaching began my awakening. That encounter with God that I had as a teenager, even after sixty-five years, continues to be the single most important event in my whole life. Having acknowledged this, it is important to raise the question of the terror, darkness, and confusion a year later.

A part of my meltdown resulted from an erroneous view of the Christian faith. At seventeen I believed the change that had occurred in me was permanent, that my only task now was to reach out to others and bring them to a faith in Christ. After sixty-five years I have learned that such an awakening is a beginning that has no end. I have also learned that I cannot preserve an experience like this for the rest of my life; life is always in motion, things are always changing and I am always changing and if I am authentic, my understanding of God is always evolving. I have learned that not only can I not hold on to an experience, I cannot go back to and reclaim it over and over. Life is movement; life flows from new challenges, new decisions and new forms. My false notion was that I could be disciplined and faithful, and this would guarantee a mature, spiritual life.

This latter expectation caused me to build a belief system that held me together while it resisted change. It was like being clothed in a coat of metal which had no room for growth and change. I viewed my new spiritual life as being complete and mature, and my task was to protect and preserve this new-found faith against all the temptations and attacks from the outside. My soul outgrew the clothes that I had been wearing, and I had to break out.

Rather than living in a capsule and protecting it with all of my energy, it would have been more conducive to a growing self if I could have seen God coming to me in the people I was meeting, the study in which I was engaging and the new feelings and intuitions that were arising in me. If I had had the courage to let go of the major transforming experience and had opened myself to the present moment, perhaps that joy and transformation could have continued. I can see this at the end of life, but I did not and could not see this vision when I was seventeen.

I tell this story so that those who have been in the light and then suddenly found themselves in fear and darkness can know that they need not despair. An awakening and a period of clarity represent not the end of growth but the beginning. New life is given us, not to grasp but to receive and then to let it pass through us. Such can be if we learn to live in this moment and then the next and the next . . .

Finally, after much suffering, I learned that I had to let go of that experience to receive what God had for me in the present moment of my life. The faith I was taught shielded me from change instead of inspiring hope that something more, something greater lay before me. On the outside I was clothed with the armor of salvation, but on the inside I was growing and changing and developing as a normal human being eighteen years of age. The old clothing just got too tight.

5. Reaching Beyond My Comfort Zone

"Before this inner dryness possessed me, I noticed the symptoms and began practices that renewed my life."

Every person has a story. Perhaps every person is a story. The parents to whom we were born, what has happened to us and how we have interpreted the various movements and transitions of our life is our story. In this short essay I explore my own life and the story that I have told myself through my interpretation of the things that have happened to me. In doing so, it is my hope that I will see more clearly the unfolding of my life through the transitions I have experienced. I have finished college and medical school and have done residency. I am now working on a specialization in neurology. I have plans to marry in a year. So at this point in my life, it seems wise to look at the family I was born into, influences that have shaped my life, and the hopes and dreams that I have for the future.

Living life at the end of a dirt road on my family's cotton and peanut farm outside Savannah formed a unique foundation for my life story. Our house was next door to my grandparents and across the field from my great aunt and uncle; I had multiple cousins, plus a twin brother and a younger brother as my siblings. For eighteen years I absorbed the lessons of life in my South Georgia community, and it was a community in every sense of the word. I moved through my school years in a place where my teachers were known and trusted by my parents, and I learned that there was a proper way of behaving toward older adults. I also absorbed, by living example, that there was a manner of treating people who were poor and different from my family. I grew up in a culture of respect and kindness for those less fortunate, and my community shaped me without my even knowing it. While these influences had a profound effect on me, there was something inside me that wanted something more, something different. I wanted to know about the world outside my South Georgia community. This restlessness or curiosity played a role in my search for a college that might fulfill some of my latent hungers. I was enamored with the idea of leaving my homogeneous, small town where all the people were really similar and going to a strange place that I knew nothing about. After some persistent convincing of my parents, my search eventually led me to McGill University in Montreal, Canada. McGill fulfilled my yearning for connection to different kinds of people from all over the world, people with different backgrounds, experiences and cultures. On the first floor of my freshman dorm were three people from Pakistan and one from a first-generation Canadian family (her parents were from Punjab, India!). Mixing my life with so many people from differing backgrounds was like breathing fresh air to me. Though it was a little scary processing what I was seeing and hearing, these strangers soon became friends as we went to classes and lived together in such a small area. As I lived in the midst of all these different people, I soon realized that they were not really so different. We all wanted many of the same things even though we came from different backgrounds; we began to see that we were really more alike than we were different. We experienced real peace and harmony in our daily life together. Why can't the world be better at this?

A Call to Medicine and the Study of Neurology

Life in college invited questions about what I was going to do with my life, and during my freshman year I had an unexpected experience that awakened my interest in studying medicine. I spent a week shadowing doctors and interns at Grady Hospital in Atlanta; this was the first time I had seen the practice of medicine up close. What impressed me most was the medical team's interaction with the patients. While following residents in their day-to-day involvement, I found myself awestruck by the way they talked with patients and encouraged the healing process. I remember one patient who was very sick and refusing medical care. Like many patients at Grady he was poor and uneducated, and he was unable to describe his physical needs. I was profoundly touched when a resident went down the hall to purchase a Sprite from the soda machine and gave it to this incommunicative patient. This simple act of kindness made the difference for that patient. Once he saw that the resident was interested enough in him to get him a soda, he responded quite differently and agreed to the recommended medical care.

Witnessing patient care, coupled with my interaction with medical students and doctors on that one significant day, was enough to convince me that I wanted to pursue medical school. Their kind attention and sensitivity toward an interloper who was seeking to find her way made me feel like part of the team. Even though I didn't understand the details of their work, it was enough for me to know I truly wanted to do this.

After a challenging yet supportive and meaningful journey through medical school, I chose to study neurology, the medical understanding of the brain and nerves. A large part of neurology is a study of those ailments that are of the neuro-degenerative type. I know that when I deal with a patient one-on-one, what I offer can be more than medical treatment. I can offer them information, diagnosis and personal care, and I can offer the healing power of kindness.

I am finished with medical school per se, and am now in my third year of specializing in neurology. Residency after medical school exposes you to something different every day, and the bread-and-butter of residency is patient care. Every morning I take care of patients in the hospital, making the rounds with an academic team. I'm now living into what I observed on that important day at Grady years ago, a day that seeded my call to this healing profession.

Work Life Meets Love Life

While I was immersed in medical studies, I met very few eligible men, so the best plan for me seemed to be shopping for a date on the Internet. The website I chose invited me to create a dating profile including my name and general information about me including where I live and what I do. It also enabled me to share things that interested me, including what I liked to read, what I liked to eat, and my particular habits. I could also research persons who had interests similar to mine. The point of writing this summary is to present oneself in enough detail to allow someone to determine if there are enough matches to make the relationship worth exploring.

This is where Karl enters the picture, as he read my profile and decided I was worth meeting! When he made contact, I read his profile and made my own judgment about whether I wanted to explore this further, and I did. Interestingly, I liked him from the first moment of our meeting, though I didn't expect him to be the man that I would eventually marry. I remember thinking that he was a fine man and was really funny. The more we talked, the more I sensed that we shared many of the same interests. Our first date was a bike ride together through Piedmont Park and Candler Park, followed by conversation over a beer. Doing something active together made it easier to connect than just sitting face-to-face for the first time and trying to find something to talk about. In reflecting on the experience, I realize that I had a really good time actually doing something together; this is a good way to get to know each other in an open, non-threatening way. Karl and I continued to see each other and engage in different activities like taking a walk, shopping, having a meal or just having a drink at a bar. Through each encounter I got to know Karl better. I discovered that he was a very open-minded person, always kind to new people and nonjudgmental in his outlook on those who were different from him. Discovering these attitudes was very important to me because I resist stereotyping individuals who are different, and I certainly did not want to be married to someone who habitually judges others. He is genuinely funny and both easy and delightful to be around.

More about Karl

Karl is also extremely hard-working; this is important to me since my work is a significant part of my life. A computer programmer and software creator, he is now self-employed and writes software for a number of large companies. The software he designs keeps records of inventory and helps to fill orders by integrating online shopping carts with products in the warehouse. Karl's success stems not only from his creativity, but also from his entrepreneurial spirit and drive. His business has grown by his being proactive about using a blog; that is the way he began to sell his software. As people learn about his work, the orders for his software grow. To further expand his work, Karl even has the courage to do some cold calling! He does quite well.

Another significant part of Karl's story involves his heritage. Though he was born in Jamaica, he was reared in Connecticut with his grandmother. While still in Jamaica, his father left his mother, and early in Karl's life his mother developed a mental illness. Because of these and other difficulties, he was sent to live with his grandmother. Nearly all his nurturing and formation came through his grandmother; he absorbed the culture of Connecticut, mingled with that of Jamaica. Though his skin is dark, I wouldn't describe him as African-American. When we began dating seriously, we shared a curiosity around our unique genetic identity, so we decided to send samples of our genes to a gene company for analysis. We learned that Karl is fifty percent African, twenty-five percent East Asian and twenty-five percent Caucasian, while I am ninety percent northern European and ten percent British.

Three and a half years have passed since that first meeting, and things have clearly progressed well in our blending of heritage, culture, and interests. Karl and I are now engaged and planning to get married in about a year. You might wonder how my parents responded to the situation when their Caucasian daughter brought home an African, Asian, Caucasian male to be introduced as my serious boyfriend. I'm happy to report that my parents were very accepting of me and Karl. They haven't shown any sign of disappointment in me, nor have they had any problem accepting Karl; my choice has not been an issue for them. They took my decision as a fact of life, and there was no pretending that it was anything else. I had met a Jamaican man who was beautiful in every way, and who manifested the kind of personal caring and dedication to hard work that I was proud of. My parents trusted me and had faith in my judgment, and because of this, I felt strongly supported. Interestingly, my grandmother had to process my decision in a different way, but after a bit of struggle, she said to my cousin, "If you raise your children not to be prejudiced, you can't be angry if they're not." She signaled to me that even older generations recognize that "the times they are a-changing."

Understanding each other is a life-long project, and there are things I need to understand about Karl and his family because their cultural dynamic is very different from mine. Likewise, he must understand me and my culture because it, too, is different from his. Yet what is more important to me than his cultural or ethnic background is who he is today and what he is seeking to become tomorrow. None of us has a choice of the family into which we are born, and none of us is conscious of the culture we are absorbing as we grow up. Children believe that the way things are in their family is the way things ought to be because it is the only way they know.

So Karl grew up in a very different family dynamic and learned a way of seeing the world from the grandmother who reared him. He had an upbringing that was almost exclusively maternal, and in his family people didn't ask probing questions; they simply did not delve into the "what" and "why" of things. This element in his family dynamic contrasts sharply with the way I was reared. In every situation I wanted to know exactly why things are the way they are; I wanted to know exactly what happened in my family and exactly where I came from. When issues arise, it is important for me to seek answers to all my questions. In my relationship with Karl, it is important for me to understand that Karl learned to accept things without questioning them, and he grew to be very forgiving and accepting of his situation. Perhaps this has made him the sensitive, caring man that he is.

While Karl does not feel it's necessary to be inquisitive and ask a lot of questions, he has to understand that my family gets involved with my life in all its aspects. It probably came as a shock to him when my family began to ask a lot of questions about why he thinks a certain way, why he has chosen his profession, and all the details of his life decisions. While some might call them nosey, I just see this as part of my culture.

Karl and I have now been living together for two and a half years, and the problem that actually comes up most frequently in our day to day living is my messiness. I am the one who leaves clothes strewn on the floor, beds unmade, and dishes in the sink. His expectations are very different. Before we began considering marriage and living together, he had a studio apartment with a desk, a chair, a loveseat, a table and a bed. No wonder his apartment was neat; he didn't have anything to strew around the house! When we began living in a two-bedroom apartment, we had an extra bedroom, a kitchen, and several closets, allowing us more things and more places to leave things. I am not the most orderly person and I don't value orderliness as Karl does, so we have issues to talk through and negotiate in order for both of us to be happy.

We have not yet discussed having children and how we will raise them. The subject does come up, most notably when we are with friends who have children or when we are out having an ice cream and observe other people's children misbehaving and how the parents deal with them. We wonder how we would act or what we would do in a similar situation. In this setting I often remark about the type of mother that I would be or how Karl would be as a father.

When we encounter children, we also think about where we want to live so that our children may grow up happy and safe. We have wondered about living in a culture that will accept mixed-race children. We don't want our children to be perceived as different; we want them to feel that they belong wherever they live. This makes it difficult to think about living in certain communities, particularly in the South, where our children may become the brunt of jokes or bullied. I would describe the school I attended in my early years as unconsciously racist. For example, we had two homecoming queens – one African-American and one Caucasian. Situations of inequality like this often made me wonder about the world beyond the borders of my community. What are people like? What is it like out there? How do those other people think and feel? Living these questions was the beginning of my awakening to a larger world. Though I truly want to live near my relatives, I don't think I could return to my home community. In light of the culture of my youth, the risk is too great that my children would be molded and influenced by feelings of rejection. This is one of the worst tragedies that could happen to any child.

More Transitions That Seeded My World View

As I look back over my life, I realize that I have had numerous influences and experiences of transition to shake me loose from the culture in which I was reared. For example, I recall a week in Boston, Massachusetts before I graduated from college. Being in that large city for a week and seeing how other people lived and what they did with their spare time was a turning point for me. Just being there and breathing the air of a different environment with so many different kinds of people living and working together was a revelation. Following that visit, I remember a restlessness that began working inside me, making me realize that the world was much larger and diverse than anything I had previously known. I realized that I could take delight in and enjoy living outside my community of origin. Though most persons I had known in my home town were good, hardworking, "salt of the earth" folks, I had a hunger for fresh experiences and new places.

My hunger took me abroad for a couple of weeks to travel in France, taking in Paris and its environs. I visited the Louvre and saw the Arc de Triomphe, an image that I had seen in my history books at school. I just loved being there; things looked and felt so different to me from my experience of living in South Georgia, the place where I had spent most of my life.

I began to realize that maybe I could actually live outside my family's farming community. As scary as it had seemed early on, I began to imagine the fun of living in a different environment and my courage grew. When I decided to move away from home and live on my own, I experienced the biggest transition I had ever faced. For me leaving the security of my parents was very difficult. Yet, if I wanted to spread my wings and try out life for myself, I needed to get far enough from my parents that they would not wonder, "What is she doing tonight? Will she be in at the appointed hour?" My parents were strict but not overbearing, yet I had moved a thousand miles from home and this decision brought an amazing degree of independence to me. It also made for a transition in my relationship with my parents. I look upon this separation as a good event; it was a good choice for me. I needed to be far enough away that I could develop my own values and plans without undue parental influence.

Being on my own opened me to the importance of making friends and developing relationships with people I could talk to about life and matters that concerned me. I began to get these insights into life; my change was subtle and incremental. Mostly, it was a gradual inward change of taking responsibility for my life.

The Inner Struggle

When I consider what I want to do or what decision I should make, I have a voice somewhere inside that speaks to me. It's almost like a dialogue where I am both asking and answering the question; it all takes place inside me. As I began to mature, I realized that I had this voice. It was something like an instinct. I just knew things and knew that I knew them. Does this make sense to you? This was the kind of voice that spoke to me before I left home. My intuition told me that if

I didn't leave now, I would never leave.

I think this inner voice was connected to a yearning for adventure. This craving for adventure must have played a part in my decision to move from the community in which I was reared to a new place and new people in another country. I recall looking at the people around me in my community, the ones who had chosen to stay in that situation and I knew I wanted something different. I believe my awareness of this stirred the urges within me to seek a different kind of life.

After making the decision to launch out into new territory, I met people along the way who engaged in pursuits that both interested and excited me. For example, the time I spent in Boston visiting a family of attorneys gave me a different picture of what I might do or where I might live. This family drew my respect, and the time that I spent with them awakened new ideas and different paths that I might take into the future. This experience made me see that no good could come out of hiding my past from myself, that is, the things that were driving me to leave my sheltered existence.

After seeing a larger world, I began to think that I would soon get bored with the kind of culture and relationships that I had known most of my life. After leaving home I felt a strong need to stay engaged and not to become complacent, yet I still faced challenges and fought burnout. Before this inner dryness possessed me, I noticed the symptoms and began practices that renewed my life. Often I turned to exercise; I worked out seriously and began to get in really good shape. To deal with my inner emptiness, I read, I exercised, and I continued to take trips to see places I had never seen before and to experience people who lived differently.

Living the Questions of My Struggles

Everyone has struggles. Though it may not be apparent to most people, I struggle with self-confidence. As I practice medicine, I am surrounded by people who are really, really brilliant; they seem to know about everything. Sometimes I find myself looking at them and saying that they seem to be much smarter than I am. Some doctors seem to have more endurance; they are able to stay up for thirty or forty hours with no sleep or rest. When I am fatigued and stressed by my work, it is really easy to get down on myself and lack a feeling of confidence. Sometimes I struggle to keep my eyes open and I wonder if it is as difficult for a man to stay alert. Does he have more strength and endurance?

I struggle with a lack of patience; when I'm working with a client who is slow or grumpy, I often feel impatient. When I encounter patients at Grady Hospital who cannot clearly express what they are feeling or what they need, I often feel very frustrated. I take a deep breath and begin to go step-by-step through the patient interview. The challenges can seem overwhelming with patients who are illiterate and unaware of their symptoms. How, for example, can a person with a brain disease communicate what he is feeling or where his pain is?

All of us struggle at times with difficult persons and needs that seem unsolvable. When facing these struggles, not only as a child growing up, but even now in my work, I have relied on my parents as a genuine source of strength and inspiration. Having a truly supportive and encouraging family continues to be a powerful resource for me. I sometimes have a religious moment when I feel their inner strength.

As I look into the future, I don't know exactly what I want to be. I do know that I would like to be a well-balanced person, have a good career and also to have bi – racial children who will be loved and appreciated. I want Karl and me to be deeply involved in their lives and engaged with them. I want us to give them a balanced life, filled with loving attention and support. Our goal will be to rear autonomous kids who can think for themselves, make their own good decisions, and be healthy-minded. I hope to remain really close to my extended family and would like for my parents and siblings to be intimately involved with our children's lives. If this is to come to pass, I realize that I have to live close enough that our children can interact with their grandparents and their aunts and uncles. If we are to have a well-balanced family, both Karl and I must have the right balance between our careers and a stable home. That balance will likely be hard to achieve, but certainly one we will work toward with purpose and determination.

6. How I Found Meaningful Work

"When I'm honest with myself, I recognize my sense of identity is still wrapped up too much in my work, though I really believe it should be wrapped around knowing that I am a child of God."

At twenty-two I felt a sense of call to get involved with social justice work. After pondering several places where my services seemed to meet their needs, I decided on an urban ministry in Atlanta. I decided to pick up all my things, leave California, and move across the country where I literally did not know a single soul.

Fast forward twenty years and I am running a nonprofit organization that builds and develops affordable rental housing. I co-founded Tapestry Development Group in Atlanta, which serves a whole continuum of low-income individuals, from homeless with special needs, to families, and seniors on a fixed income.

In some small way I hope that what we do makes a difference in the world. My life is one enormously blessed with resources, most of which I didn't have any control over -- the color of my skin, the middle class family I was born into, and the culture and values that influenced my childhood. In a mysterious and beautiful way, this all blended together to spark a need in me to give back to others.

As I reflect on those early days of landing in this southern city, I remember feeling major culture shock as I adjusted to life in the inner city. Though I thought I was prepared, there was no way to avoid the shock I experienced living through daily life immersed in a culture I did not understand. Being around mostly low-income African Americans was very new for me, so I had to embrace change in order to adapt. My cultural habits had to change, including language, values, and expectations.

The Deep South was a very different culture from the West Coast. Life in the South moved at a much slower pace. People were much more friendly and hospitable than what I was accustomed to in California. There were dress codes that I wasn't aware of, having grown up as a young woman in Los Angeles. I remember going to a jazz club one evening and realizing I was not accepted because I wore pants. I have to say that was one major change, yet in spite of the difficulties, I thrived on the changes I was making. Engaging fully in inner-city life in the South was a fast and good teacher, and I loved it! I believed I was called to be there, even though the transition was very, very challenging and sometimes painful.

As I began my work life within the urban ministry that drew me to Atlanta, I felt very disconnected. I think the overarching word that describes me and my first years of work here is lonely. I needed a community, and as I began to get deeper into my work with housing and homelessness, I realized that the people around me had a sense of community. They were drawn together because they were working seriously for social justice, but everyone engaged in this work already had their own friends and their own sense of community. I invested a lot of energy figuring out how I could become part of the community. I realized I had not found a new church family, and church is where I had known community in California. I made a strategic decision to find a church where the majority of the people were African-American. It was important to me to understand the struggles faced by the people I was seeking to help, so besides living and working in the community of majority African-Americans, I also began to worship with people who looked different from me. We all shared a similar faith, and this helped me adjust to life outside my comfort zone.

Finding new friends who were about my age and status in life was hard. A small group of people reached out to me, and I eventually gained courage to get actively involved in structured programs to meet people. I heard about a program that paired people like me with elderly persons, mostly women who had low incomes and lived in inner-city neighborhoods. It was the Adopt A Grandparent Program, part of the urban ministry that I was involved with. Its purpose was to develop friendships and build relationships with persons you would not normally meet. I feel like God chose a very special person for me. I was connected with Agnes, a sixty-two- year-old woman from South Africa, and I began to discover the richness of my new relationship with a black woman who had raised seven children during the apartheid era.

I learned that Agnes moved to Atlanta the same year that I did – 1994. She was married at the time, but she later divorced in Atlanta before I met her. Agnes was not a refugee; she was an immigrant, but other than her ex-husband, she had no other family in the United States.

Agnes and I entered into a lovely, beautiful friendship where I felt that she had truly adopted me as her child and I adopted her as my grandmother. I had no other family in Georgia, and we were a wonderful fit. I spent time with her: I helped her pay bills and her taxes, and I also drove her to appointments in my car. Agnes journeyed with me into some very challenging parts of my life, as this was a time when my mother was in ill health in California. We listened to each other and helped one another, and we shared both the joys and sorrows of life. I fondly remember when Agnes decided to become an American citizen. I helped her through the application process and the test. What a joy to be able to celebrate with her the day she was sworn in as an American citizen!

Just two years ago, I helped Agnes move back to South Africa. She had retired and wanted to return to be with her family. I miss her terribly, but thanks to modern technology, we stay in touch both through emails and free texting.

Interestingly, I had traveled to South Africa before I ever met Agnes. After completing graduate studies in city planning at Georgia Tech, I felt better prepared for the vision and vocational call that was coming to me. With a sense of strength and confidence, I traveled to South Africa to spend four months volunteering with people who were deeply committed to diversity and to issues of poverty, homelessness, and injustice. After four months, I returned to Atlanta and found a position doing exactly what I wanted to do – developing affordable rental housing for a nonprofit organization. This experience, coupled with my relationship with Agnes, brings an enduring sense of connection to South Africa.

With a renewed sense of God's call to my work, I felt energized by my role within this large nonprofit organization dedicated to developing and managing rental housing for low-income families. Opening possibilities for affordable housing involves various dimensions and a variety of skills. I was not only connecting with homeless people with special needs, but I was also managing large projects alongside architects, contractors, and surveyors. Working with this diverse group of people required using my business skills for a charitable purpose. I not only managed all the work of the development team, I also secured the financing and oversaw the closing of all the projects. Construction and rehabilitation of these properties allowed me to use the skills God has graced me with, so do you see why I loved my work? I joyously invested my energy and experience in helping make life better for marginalized people. I was making a difference in their lives by opening new possibilities through the housing and the support services we provided.

Though my work was truly rewarding, it was also very challenging. I was new to the whole world of real estate finance, and directing large teams of people was a major shift for me. At times I felt like I didn't know what I was doing. My insecurities bubbled up, and voices in my head began to say, "You don't have enough smarts to do this, or you don't have enough skills to do that." What kept me going through the tough times was the subtle and mysterious voice of God somehow showing me that this is where I needed to be. I felt like I had to stick with it, keep learning, and persist through the tough times.

So how did I deal with my insecurities? As I reflect, I see how much I have grown over the last sixteen years. My coping mechanism back then was to suppress my insecurities and just move forward. I don't think I was really aware enough to dig deeply, sort things through, and learn how to recover. I was blocked by a lot of self-judgment; as a self-described perfectionist, I also became an obsessive workaholic. I wasn't open to the grace that comes with self-acceptance and mindful awareness. By becoming more mindful over time, I'm now able to intentionally be open to change so that my identity is not so closely aligned with my work performance. I realize now I often jumped into my work whole hog as a way to feel better about myself.

By cultivating greater self-acceptance and awareness, I was able to make wise decisions about my career path when the nonprofit I had been part of for more than twelve years began to shift priorities. The organization made a conscious decision to focus on managing our existing projects and let go of new development. I was and still am a developer at heart, a deal junkie of sorts. When I looked at the landscape, I knew that affordable housing development was still in my DNA. My spirit sensed a continued need for a nonprofit, mission-minded developer in Atlanta. I had skills that could be best directed in a mission-driven organization, so I co-founded Tapestry Development Group four years ago.

A combination of hard work and mostly God's grace helped grow this new organization through challenges, even when the odds were against us. It was 2010 during the worst recession of my lifetime, and the Atlanta real estate market was particularly shattered. My colleagues and I worked diligently to be both entrepreneurial and assertive in looking for new development opportunities.

Thankfully opportunities seemed to just come down to us like manna from heaven, yet fear of failure continues to creep in. When I'm honest with myself, I recognize my sense of identity is still wrapped up too much in my work, though I really believe it should be wrapped around knowing that I am a child of God. My struggles multiplied through a challenging separation from a business partner. In looking back I now see that there were significant lessons to learn through the suffering endured in this difficult work relationship. One of the biggest gifts was in recognizing that I didn't have to worry about what others think of me.

I never call myself a risk-taker, yet my entrepreneurial spirit was evident through my journey in this mission-focused career, especially the period of my life when I started Tapestry. Growing up, I was always the shy one, yet as I look back on my adult life I can see very distinct periods when I took some major risks. I didn't really think about all of the major consequences; I just jumped in full bore with a sense of adventure in trying something new. My adventurous spirit also influenced other choices, like getting married and choosing to buy a house in the inner city in a troubled neighborhood. My intention was much the same as my intention for going to South Africa: I wanted to become part of the community with the hope of making a difference. Our risk-taking continued when my husband and I welcomed a foster son into our home. He was with us for two years before we began having our own biological children, and even though he no longer lives with us, we feel very blessed that he is still in our lives.

I'm in a period of discernment right now, wondering what's next for my career. In one way I feel ready to move on to something new and am pondering being part of a large corporation. Will this allow me to have an even greater impact by encouraging people within the corporation to be more socially responsible? Perhaps this will feed all of my desire and ambition for impact on a wider scale to the under-resourced areas of our world. At the same time I'm feeling pulled to dial back my career ambitions. I'm thinking very seriously about just working part-time so that I can spend more time with my children, my elderly parents, my husband. It's been an interesting interior journey because it raises all sorts of issues about where I get my identity and how much I receive my identity from the work I do. The struggle I face is in dealing with my fears of the unknown. I'm living the "what if" questions. What if my vocation really is to spend more time as a mom, as a daughter, as a wife? What if I'm not successful on a new path? Can I really embrace knowing that my identity is not tied to what I do, but rather to who I am as a child of God? This is true regardless of where I invest my gifts and skills.

As I turn forty-two this week, I feel a little bit as if I'm in a midlife crisis, though it is not a crisis of faith. I feel very secure in my relationship with God, and that is comforting. At least as I'm walking in the darkness, I sense that I am confronting a lot of fears about the unknown. As I consider my next path and my purpose in life and work, I realize that new decisions will bring significant changes. Choosing to work part-time will clearly have a financial impact, and less income brings fear that I won't be able to step back later in life because I won't have enough retirement savings. All these decisions impact family dynamics, and while my situation may be atypical, I also sense that I'm not alone in my fears and questioning. Fortunately, along with the questions and sense of fear about the future, I also have a sense of good things to come.

One of the most helpful resources for navigating this time of transition is a small group of very dear friends, not all of whom live here in Atlanta. I call this trusted group my "soul friends" because I can talk with them about deep matters of the heart and soul. I have developed these relationships over twenty years, and since most in the group are ten to fifteen years older than me, they are a little farther along the journey than I am. They remind me that it's okay to have questions, and it's okay to take risks. Life is a marathon, not a sprint. Life can also be viewed as book, and I can't live all the chapters at once. Each distinct chapter offers challenges and opportunities.

I think the word companion is perfect to describe these soul friends. They are not telling me what to do, but rather they are walking alongside me, wondering with me. Rather than say "here is what you should do and I know because I've lived this," they reassure me about the possibilities and the mystery of life. My friends have helped me to recognize that we don't have all the answers, and we don't know the future. All I can do is take a step forward and realize that this is a phase. I may choose to step back from my career full time now, but that doesn't mean it will always be this way.

One of my soul friends shared something recently that has made a world of difference to me. Instead of giving me advice, she simply shared her personal experience. She noted that as a mother and wife, she came to see that she was the anchor of her home. At the same time she was the anchor in her role as senior pastor of a church. Trying to be an anchor in two places was more than she felt she could do at that point in her life, so after pausing to reflect, she stepped back and became more part-time at her church. She ended up in a co-pastor role where she could share responsibility at church and spend less time in her actual work there. Making that choice led her to a sense of balance or wholeness. By sharing her experience, my soul friend articulated for me the stirrings of my own heart. Were my feelings of divided allegiance getting to the point of making me ineffective in both spheres, or at least less effective than I want to be? I'm struck by the combination of reflecting on what I was sensing in my life, sharing with a trusted friend, and then contemplating the questions that emerged. These seemed to blend together, allowing me to live more fully into possibilities for healing and wholeness.

One of the biggest gifts in discovering what I would call a more contemplative spirituality comes from accepting mystery and the reality of not knowing all the answers in life. I don't know exactly where my wanderings are going related to my career, and especially as it relates to working part-time. If I dial back from my current work, will I just get restless and start dreaming up a new business or ministry that I want to be involved with? I'm actually very comfortable right now in the unknowing of what is next. I don't know how much longer I'll feel that way, but at the moment it feels like that's where I'm supposed to be. A pastor friend recently offered me a good piece of advice when I asked him how he counsels people when they're considering transitions in their vocation. He offered something so simple yet very profound for me. Just wake up each morning and ask God what's next. Then don't wait for an answer right away. Simply posing the question opens me to accept the wondering and waiting even as I realize it is not likely that answer will come in a very short day or week or two. There is value in continuing to ask the question, because when the answer does arise, I will know it through the emotional and spiritual work I'm personally doing as I open and live the questions. So I wake up and ask God what's next without assuming that I'm going to get an answer. The discipline of being mindful and asking the question is very helpful for me.

I wholeheartedly believe that this good internal work is what I need to do to grow as a person. It is the wondering that has forced me to confront my fear, to realize that my mind is conditioned to automatically go to the worst-case scenario. Yet as I bring it back to the present moment, I recognize that the worst doesn't always happen. This process helps me see that I don't need to always go there.

I'm also reading this really powerful book by Brene Brown entitled *Daring Greatly: How the Courage to Be Vulnerable Transforms the Way We Live, Love, Parent, and Lead*. Brown's research on living a wholehearted life is showing that those people who live more wholehearted, joyful lives are those who allow themselves to be vulnerable. It is in being open and honest with ourselves and others that we are able to connect. I believe this journey of wondering what's next for me has allowed me to connect more deeply with companions and friends along the journey. That's been a gift in and of itself, and hopefully my connection with God will also deepen through this. I sense that this vulnerable time will help me embrace joy and become a more durable, openhearted person.

While I've been a Christian since I was a young child, I notice now a deep new sense of trust and the possibility of letting go of my fear of the unknown. In Christ, I can get away from striving so much to find my identity in my work. I have a very clear sense of God's grace, even in my woundedness and my not knowing. I don't need to know the answers, and I can allow the changes to come through Christ. It sounds so simple, yet this opens me to healthy, wholehearted decisions. I have this image of clinging to Jesus the way you would cling to a raft. My raft is floating along now, and it brings a lot of comfort to know that I'm not in control. I'm not changing myself; I'm opening and allowing Jesus to change me. As I live the questions, I trust that I will get to the place where I need to be because of His grace.

7. Finding Myself through a Serious Illness

*"Maybe the foundation for resilience is in knowing
who you are and knowing you're not alone."*

Who I am now and everything I have become occurred through my experience with a life-threatening illness. Before being diagnosed, I was some loser teenage guy without any idea of who I really was as a person. At seventeen or eighteen I wonder if anyone has any idea or sense of who he or she is! It's a mystery to me how something so terrible can bring about such wonderful transitions that connect who you are with what you do. It was only through a time of painful transition that I came to know myself and to discover what I wanted to do with my life. Before living through this pain and uncertainty, I thought that I wanted to be an ESPN sports anchor. When I took the things I learned as a patient through major treatment and hospitalizations, my life's vision was changed to the medical field.

As I reflect on my transition from transplant patient to healing professional, I'm humbled and grateful to now be a physician's assistant (PA) caring for children and families as they prepare for the difficult journey through bone marrow transplant.

Facing the Diagnosis
My beginning to pass through this transition came during my senior year in high school. I found myself wondering why, as a student athlete, I was feeling increasingly exhausted. Sleeping a lot and unable to exercise, I was fast becoming an out of shape teenager. While I was getting lazy, fat and playing too many video games, a random doctor's appointment and a routine check-up got my attention. Tests revealed that my blood counts were really off. My red blood cell count was 7 or 8 where it should have been in the 14-15 range, and my white cell count, the cells that fight off infection, were less than one rather than the normal 4.5-12 range. My platelets, which are the cells that

stop bleeding when you get cut, were down in the 20-30 range and they should be over 150,000! My doctor repeated the test because my numbers were so wacky. These variations were highly irregular, especially for a teenager. He wanted to make sure it wasn't a lab error or another person's sample. They repeated the test and my numbers were still way off, so I was sent to an adult hematologist.

A significant point of transition came when the adult hematologist said, "Listen, I don't know if you noticed, but all the people in the waiting room are fifty, sixty, seventy years old and you're eighteen. I'm happy to take care of you, but I don't know if I'm really equipped. I think you might be better served by seeing someone at the children's hospital." That moment of honesty was huge in my journey and was one of the most important medical decisions made for me as a person. My doctor's awareness that I fit in the pediatric world a lot better than I did with the adult world registered as a "full check" in caring for me as a whole person. I was right on the edge where my doctor could have been an adult hematologist, but the choice to put me in the pediatric world put me on the path that I'm following today.

At the children's hospital I was diagnosed with myelodysplastic syndrome (MDS), a pre-leukemia status and definitely a disease not much fun to have! With this disease you experience the failure of all your bone marrow cells, and the only treatment for that is a bone marrow transplant. Though it is a disease that you cannot live with for a long time, my condition was not acutely dangerous. At the time, my illness was deemed stable enough for me to finish high school before starting down the transplant road. I even began college with the hope that I could delay treatment a bit longer.

Being thrown into the unknown world of illness and treatment options was terrifying. Hearing your name in the same sentence with words like leukemia and cancer – that's pretty scary! Luckily, my mother was not only a wonderful nurse; she was also a pretty strong woman. She was a source of inspiration throughout my whole illness and was always there for me. She kept up a strong exterior even though I know she was melting on the inside. Her strength was really important to me; from her I learned how to be that for my own patients.

The Intensity and Darkness of Transplant

The transplant period is very intense and not something to be done lightly. People in my condition are sick for a long period of time and in most cases face death. I had a couple of those, and I feel lucky that I made it through. These encounters shaped who I am. The struggle can really move you toward being a better person. Unfortunately, in a lot of cases, through no fault of their own, some people are destroyed by adversity or illness. I was one of the lucky ones to make it out on the other side and to gain a different outlook on the amazing journey we call life.

During my time of severe illness, all the other things in my life seemed to get washed away and I was left with my true self. I believe that if we have the strength to honestly look at ourselves when everything else is gone, that's when we can grow as a person. It's not an easy thing to do, and we can't do it alone. I think I was only able to accept my situation because of the relationship I had with my mom, my dad, my family, and my good friends. I now recognize that throughout my life adversity has brought me closer to people. Two friends in particular come to mind who have drawn closer to me and I to them through these difficult experiences.

Healing Moments That Build Strength Within

During the transplant period I not only relied on my mom and my friends but, more importantly, the nursing and medical staff who took care of me. They all helped me build a stronger faith in myself and in the medical treatment I was receiving. Nothing helps me like belief in myself when I'm going through a tough time. I observe others who find this strength in their religion, but I was never really a religious person. Maybe religion is simply a tool to help the person know and build the inner self, and it is in strengthening what lies within where the healing comes. The more I work with other patients going through similar experiences to mine, the more I know that it's not possible to move through these life-threatening situations without confidence in yourself. Illness is something you must walk through yourself, even though the relationships with other people and your religious faith may help strengthen you. I realize that you must rely on yourself, because what happens when there is no one else around to help you?

Maybe knowing yourself opens you to those significant relationships that allow you to also rely on others in healing and healthy ways. I think in the end if you don't have that strong, strong core, then you're really going to struggle mightily and may not come out with the improvement in yourself that I was lucky to experience.

As I reflect on how I came to connect with my strong core, it seems that moments of experience and relationship combined to open me to knowing that I could endure whatever came my way. I remember several particularly poignant moments when I first found out I had myelodysplastic syndrome (MDS).

Upon diagnosing my MDS and knowing there's no mild way to treat this disease, the medical staff made their visit to my hospital room. I was suddenly gripped by fear as I saw the gravity of the diagnosis on their faces. I heard it in their voices as they delivered the bad news; in that moment I felt most scared. And when they left the room, I clearly remember my mom struggling with her own fear. I caught a fleeting glimpse of the terror on her face, but when she looked at me, she put on her strongest expression. Even now, my heart is filled with emotion when I recall her hug that transformed my fear into courage. It was the strongest hug I've ever had! She turned toward me with the confidence that we were going to make it through. That moment of courage and hope set the tone for the rest of the journey. Seeing my mom demonstrating strength and knowing she wasn't going to let this get her down, turned me in the right direction. For strength and courage, I can always return to that moment – knowing my mom had my back. I can only imagine how hard it was for her to be strong and find courage, especially in the toughest moments when her fear was very real.

Though there's not a switch you can flip to go from being really scared to being really courageous, there are clearly moments to build on. That was my big *OK, here I am, moment. That moment I knew that I've got the strength to move on to the next stage.* With the help of the people behind me, caring for me, each stage I got through built my core strength even more.

My mom has always been right there for me . . . and with the biggest smile she could put on and the best joking moment she could pull out. Humor is just an amazing gift, and something that clearly helped me through.   Having a good attitude and trying to find humor even in the most ridiculous moments was really powerful.

Though I'm not a religious person, I can't even tell you how many people came to me and said, *"You're on the prayer list at church."* Wow! Although I'm not sure what that means, I do know it means a lot to have friends who care enough to let you know they care. That's really cool. I don't think you have to participate in everyone's belief system to draw courage from their caring. Everyone tries in different ways to handle these situations. Knowing that people care enough to mention this to me and let me know they were thinking about me really meant a lot.

That said, it's hard for me to figure out where inner strength comes from and how there's a difference in religious and spiritual beliefs.   I don't know if one thing is more important than the other, but when people care for you, it seems to be something you feel rather than what you believe.   It's a mystery, and I don't know where that inner belief in yourself comes from. It's really ambiguous and there's not one thing that I can specifically point to and say, *that's it.* These deep inner feelings and relationships with others are too deep for words. I have not been able to grasp where that strength comes from, but I feel it in tender moments like that moment with my mom when I was first diagnosed. I also feel it in funny moments.

Another powerful moment sticks in my mind.   I was extremely sick after taking one of the essential drugs before my transplant. My blood pressure was too low, and the staff was pumping in blood and fluids. Disoriented and confused, I didn't know where I was, but I knew there were a lot of things going on around me. I sensed that my heart was beating so hard that I could feel my pulse in my gums. I was feeling awful, and when I recognized the nurse working with me, I asked, "Am I gonna die today?"   I remember her eyes and her mouth so clearly when she looked at me and said, "Absolutely not, Darren! We've got this under control and you're not gonna die today." What an amazing thing when I consider the courage she evoked in me by genuinely conveying, "No! I've got you, and we're gonna make sure you come through this!"   Moments like that are just incredible in my memory. I needed reassurance when I was overwhelmed with conflicted thoughts and emotions. It's amazing how just one person, one moment, can shift my mind to say, "Okay, get back on track." So I never underestimate the power of a moment, a connection or a gesture.

What is good medicine?

The power of one person and one moment is revealed to me now as I work with patients. There are hundreds of different kinds of pain that people go through – like losing their parents at an early age or being diagnosed with a life-threatening illness. No matter what they are going through. it seems that we all need people around us to help bolster our confidence and to remind us that we're strong enough to make it through life. I think that's a really cool thing about being human. Each of us needs other people to make it through life!

There were definitely times of intense physical pain when I went through chemotherapy, but physical pain is different from emotional pain. The toll that the emotional pain took on me was actually harder than the physical pain caused by changes going on in my body. When I was having the transplant, I had a button that delivered narcotics on demand, which eased my physical pain. It was the emotional pain of dealing with the illness that caused my deeper suffering; I had no button I could push to get through the emotional pain. Sometimes people confuse emotional pain with physical pain, and I was able to strengthen my "emotional muscles" through suffering.

The time after the transplant is the hardest part, and that's when you are the sickest. The sickness usually lasts for about three months, but for me it took a good bit longer. It was six to eight months before I was really back to my normal self. After six months when I thought about quitting, I'd simply look back and say to myself, *"Look at all I've accomplished and all this suffering I've endured. I can't stop now! Quitting wouldn't make any sense."* I built up both endurance and patience by living through the precarious changes, from sitting in waiting rooms, from going through all sorts of tests and infusions. Each test I ticked off made the next one a little easier, and each time I got a boost of confidence in myself. I kept saying, *"I've been through all this. What's another few weeks, what's another day, what's another infusion?"* There's a powerful lesson in moving through any difficult transition. Knowing I can find the strength to press on has really been helpful to me in daily life. Push forward, one moment at a time.

How can you go through something like that and not be confident in yourself? The answer to this question seems pretty simple to me. Other good things have come out of this terrible illness that have changed me for the better. The people who took care of me really empowered me to care deeply for other people. I can't recall who I was before transplant, but now I am certainly a more caring human being and a lot more confident as a person. During my illness I encountered so many different people and so many different situations, that it seems like my ability to interact with others greatly increased.

It's hard to look back and see exactly what made my experience successful and why I was able to move through it more positively than some others. The main thing seems to be the relationships, whether it was those people who were around me every step of the way or those who came in for just a moment. Every little bit counted. I wonder if some people plainly don't know how to take being cared for. Why was it so easy for me to rely on others? Maybe it was because I had a solid upbringing with loving parents and great brothers. I don't know. That's something I haven't been able to figure out. Why is it easier for some of us to rely on others and let go of our independence? I guess it's about allowing yourself to be in the moment and take in the moment as it comes. This allows me to take life as it unfolds. Is this something that I built up or was I able to do that before my illness? It goes back to that mystery of discovering who you are and that piece of yourself that is hard to pinpoint in words. I will call it the mystery of being me.

The lessons are within me, yet there's so much to ponder. Why do some of us come through tough transitions stronger and more open, more loving, more caring? Others go another way? I don't know, yet I keep going back to the importance of relationships, like the nurses who took care of me when I was really my sickest. They would sit at my bedside for hours and look at me or talk with me or just be with me. Imagine at two o'clock in the morning being willing to talk to me about anything! The caring and connection I felt is just unreal to me. That's why I decided to do what I do! And yet I still don't know why some are able to take in caring and some are not. I wish I had an answer. I could write an awesome book about it!

Real Connection Is Good Medicine

When most of us think of good medicine, we think of prescribing the right drugs, taking vital signs and other such actions. These basics may be necessary, but I now think the key to providing really good medical care is through an emotional connection. When I think about my experience, I don't think about that time they prescribed a pill that made me feel better. The things I remember most are those crucial moments of connection, like when that nurse told me I wasn't going to die. Or those healing moments when I was sickest and the nurse was sitting at my bedside for hours just shooting the breeze so I would feel more comfortable. Even at two in the morning! That's really what it means to provide great medical care. Being emotionally invested in people and wanting what's best for them. It may come out in the process of prescribing the right drugs and getting to the bottom of the illness, but especially in the field I'm in now, it's really more about emotional connection than anything else. It's about doing things that allow patients to believe that you care about them, and that makes the whole medical interaction much easier.

I was talking to a doctor recently about the physical exams and how they've become less and less personal. We can get so invested in all these tests and numbers and forget how important it is to touch our patients. I know what it feels like to touch them and sense when they really let you in. That genuine touch breaks down barriers and allows me to see the person behind the diagnosis. I think that's the key to really good medicine. It's in paying attention to the emotional level and embracing the whole person. That's what I try to do on a daily basis as a PA - get to know people, touch them and care for them.

I work on the pediatric wing, and it's sad in many ways. It seems to me the kids who really struggle the most are the kids whose parents don't seem to get it, don't realize that they need caring and love and attention from them. The kids who have a caring parent do a lot better. So what can I do for those kids who don't seem to have the best support from their moms and dads? How can a six- or eight-year-old figure out life if they don't have someone behind them pushing them along? In those situations I have to do my best to show them there are people who care. When I can help them feel caring, it can make a huge difference. It doesn't have to be a parent. It can be a brother or a friend or anyone who is connected and interested. If kids don't have at least one person behind them who really cares, then it's hard for them to make it. It's easy for me to see these things because I know how important it is to have that encouraging friend or family member. We all need someone to care and reassure us in our darkest hours. We need to know that someone is behind us, someone is there rooting for us and helping to pull us through. Caring is that significant!

And for me, it's also about continuing to care for myself, not in a selfish way, but in a way that makes it possible for me to connect with my very sick patients. This allows me to bring healing without my burning out or turning bitter. I've spent hours crying with patients and families, and it's hard; though if I stop trying to make the emotional connection, I may as well hang it up. I just won't be able to be an efficient and useful provider.

Families do rely on me as a source of strength because they know that I have been through it. This makes it especially hard for me when things go wrong. I worry that I gave them a false hope; yet my own illness taught me that I can't dwell on every terrible thing that happens in life. That attitude makes for a miserable, sad person. So feeling it and moving through it is a tool I learned. If I stay sad about every little thing and keep carrying it on my back, life gets too heavy and I'm good for nothing to anyone. It's like I've built up this emotional ability to close old doors and walk through new ones. In the moment I can be emotional and really feel connected to patients; then when I leave that situation I'm able to close it down so that I can be open to the next encounter. So that tool is useful . . . and so is a good beer! And I have to go back to my friends and people who are there for me when I'm not at work. My friends help me remember that in times of adversity if you think you can control everything, then you will fail and probably fail pretty hard. My friends also help me remember to laugh.

Laughter Is Good Medicine!

A good sense of humor is one of my calling cards. When I started on the pediatric unit, I soon noted that the atmosphere got light-hearted when I was around. You can't go through life thinking everything is so serious that you can do nothing but frown. Even when people are in the darkest times going through transplant and having a lot of

GI issues, humor can carry them through.   Gastro-intestinal issues are common in transplant patients, and I remember one time a few friends were with me in the hospital and they gave me some pudding. The docs were always collecting my stool because it's an important indicator of certain kinds of illness. Lovely! So I thought it would be really cute if I stuffed the pudding in the collection bag in front of all my friends. I happened to have this really cute, young nurse. She came in and saw the bag full of something, and she really didn't know what to do.   I could tell she didn't want to bring it up with all my friends present, and I eventually confessed that it was just pudding. I guess you had to be there to get the full effect, but we all laughed hysterically. Even in the darkest moments, it's really important to see the levity in ordinary things, so I try my best to laugh everyday.   Laughter is good medicine, and humor can dissolve the pain of any situation.

My daily work places me around situations of heaviness and even death, so bringing a light heart to all of it helps.   I have told my brother that when I die, I want to have a FUN-eral rather than a funeral. I want it to be more about a celebration of my life rather than mourning my death.   Rather than having a bunch of people sit around and cry, I hope my friends will tell stories and remember when Darren did this or remember the time we were all together laughing about something else.   I hope my FUN-eral is about good beer, good memories, and good people. I want the people I love to lean into the goodness instead of the sadness.

Looking at Life a Different Way

Sadly, I deal with kids who die at six or eight years old or an adult who dies at thirty-five and is a father of young kids – cases where parents lose a child and where a child loses a parent. It's sad, and it's hard to quantify the sadness.   Death happens and for too many it happens sooner rather than later. I am around it daily. It's not an easy thing to deal with, and my experience of being close to death has changed the way I think about it. Rather than dwell on fear of death, I focus on the love of life! I feel like I have a lot more things to do in my life, so I'd be disappointed if death happens sooner rather than later. That said, I still have to think about all the things I've done in life rather than all the things I could have done. It's hard to look at death without making it a sad occasion, but I think we have to look at it from a different perspective; otherwise, we never get on with life. Maybe it's about accepting death as a part of life.

One of the gifts that some are able to take away from difficult or sad situations is to look at life in a different way. I also think it's unfortunate that it takes loss to bring out what matters most in life. As I reflect on the ups and downs in my life, I realize what a gift it is to be able to step back and really see what matters. And also to realize that there are no magic or easy answers. We can't settle for easy answers that lead us to say, "Oh, now I get it! I know I can make it through this." It's not like that; it's not an on and off switch; it takes time and effort.

I am amazed when I realize that my illness opened me to who I am, personally and professionally. The lessons I learned are powerful, deeply appreciated gifts. Today I know that we're not in it alone, and we don't need to be afraid to ask for help. I think that human beings are amazing in the way they give to others. I think that's really cool about us. You may see that bad things are happening all around, but the human spirit is pretty damn cool! If we open ourselves to others and allow them in, we allow them to help us when things seem dire.

And it's not easy. Opening yourself up is also about opening the real you to who you really are, inside and out. This sometimes brings anger and other difficult emotions, but if we are willing to give it a shot and work with what we feel, we can work at not becoming bitter, even in the worst situations.

All this comes through the human spirit. I wonder how to stay connected to that spirit, to who I am really meant to be? My illness made the difference between knowing who I am and not knowing who I am. Opening up and reflecting inward, that's a practice that needs to continue throughout life. As a seventeen-year-old I didn't really give that much thought . . . until I got sick. Maybe the foundation for resilience is in knowing who you are and knowing you're not alone. Growing to know my own identity and integrity is essentially how I've been able to take my situation and thrive as a person, yet it didn't come easy, that's for sure.

8. Raising Children: Insights from a Mother's View

"When parents and teachers work together to encourage self-awareness, this helps children thrive and learn to navigate transitions."

What a privilege to be a woman and then to be a mother. Nothing quite compares with that experience! I am fortunate to be the mother of two children, both boys. I suppose none of us feels adequate for the tasks of motherhood, but I have tried to learn all that I could and then do my best to rear my children to be good persons and contributors to society. Reflecting on memories of learning and growing with my children, and also with the young children that I have taught, has been a delightful experience. Telling my story is fulfilling to me, and I hope that it will provide insight and encouragement to other mothers and fathers.

Something that I had not seriously considered before becoming a mother was that from birth to age twelve, infants go through dozens of transitions. Pediatric charts reveal that every couple of weeks some type of transition occurs – physical, mental or emotional. When I consider these enormous changes and adjustments, it seems to me that it truly takes a whole tribe to raise children these days. As a new parent I needed both care and guidance, and having a child was the first time I faced the reality that I was not in control of my life.

While children go through numerous changes, I pause to underscore the fact that women also go through significant changes on the path to becoming a mother. Here I was a single young woman, who fell in love, joined herself to a good husband, got pregnant, carried the fetus for nine long months, labored in the hospital to give birth to a boy and then took him home with me. Believe me when I tell you that during that period, I went through a lot of changes myself. And, every time my child changed, I had to change to respond to his needs. So it's not only kids who are changing, but also those who birth them and care for them.

As an adult I know that I, too, went through all the transitions that my children faced, yet I really can't recall how, as a child, I handled them. Who does remember being unable to hold her head up or to focus her vision? Who recalls learning that even if a person leaves the room, she or he still exists? When I left the room when my child was young, he cried because he was not sure that I would return. I trust I, too, cried when my mother left the room, and it helps me to know this.

I think that all these changes in the early months are so dramatic that the newborn needs constant physical contact with both mom and dad. When my firstborn was about six weeks old, we went to the zoo. Even though we were outside and in a fun place, my son would not stop crying. Being a new mom, I didn't know if he was still hungry, although I had just fed him. It was Labor Day weekend and we were in Knoxville, Tennessee where it was pretty hot in early September. Because I couldn't quiet him, I decided that he was hot, so I gave my husband a washcloth and asked him to wet it while I took off all of the baby's clothes. When my husband returned with the wet cloth, my son was in his diaper only. I put the cool washcloth on his head and immediately he stopped crying.

That day I began to learn to trust the voice that whispers softly and persistently in my head. Over time, I have learned to listen to that little voice of intuition, which I call the "Mommy Voice." When that intuitive voice speaks to me, I listen to it because I want to sense what my children need. I have found these impressions invaluable, and even when my intuitions have not been completely accurate, I still feel empowered to investigate the issue and get it resolved.

In another instance, I had to deal with my three-year-old son who did not play much one day; he simply had low energy. He did not eat much that day either. He had no fever or congestion or symptoms of any kind, yet I knew there was something wrong. By the end of the day, I told my husband that I was planning to take him to the pediatrician the next morning. My husband probably said to himself, "Okay, she's listening to the little voice in the back of her head and I won't argue with it." The next morning when my son woke up, he had a rash on his stomach. It turned out that my child had scarlet fever.

It is so important to learn the language of your child and to interpret what his or her actions are speaking. Mothers must learn to listen to their children's language spoken through their play, their eating habits, sleep, nonverbal movements, and more. A mother's relationship with her child is very intimate; sometimes it feels symbiotic, so powerful it is difficult to describe in words.

The physical connection is certainly evident during pregnancy, yet I was surprised how physically engaged I was in the act of caring for my infant. If you breast feed, you are on duty all day and all night; if you have had this experience, you know what I'm talking about. My body reacted to my baby's every cry and coo. Of course I thought I would fall in love with my child and that I would want to do anything for him. I didn't realize that love would happen on a cellular level!

I think I had a really hard time adjusting when I first became a mom because I was so goal-oriented: these are the steps you follow and then you will achieve what you desire. That's not really how babies grow; they don't respond like predictable machines. A goal-oriented approach is not always the best for dealing with your child. The child has to do the growing; as a parent I provide the support. My first maternity leave was so intense; I decided with my second child to be more conscious of expectations for myself. I had to remember to take care of myself in order to care for another, so I made sure that I brushed my teeth and got my rest. Taking care of oneself seems like such an obvious thing, but I seriously had to work at it. When I took time for myself, I was much more capable of responding appropriately to the needs of my infant. Once I learned to focus on the present need and acknowledged my own limits, things between me and my infant went much smoother.

A respected authority on children told me to treat a child's experience and his emotions as valid. Even if in my adult wisdom, I don't see the situation the same way he does, I must treat his experiences with respect and empathy. The loud noise of a vacuum cleaner doesn't jolt me into a "fight or flight" adrenaline rush, but to a child it can feel life-threatening. Just because the child isn't in actual danger doesn't make his experience any less real. It is real to him, so when I react to his experience, I should do so with respect and empathy. Both qualities are foundational to unconditional love.

A Teacher's Perspective. . . Pause before Rushing In to Fix!

Often just taking the time simply to observe a child's behavior can be really helpful. Instead of rushing in to "fix" situations for a child, sit back and watch and let him or her attempt to figure it out. When teaching Pre-Kindergarten, I remember a time when my class was fascinated with this *Rush Hour* game – an independent activity for one person. While I was talking with a parent after school, her son intensely watched another child playing *Rush Hour*. He asked if he could play. The other boy replied, "No, I'm busy with this. You'll have to wait!" Things quickly escalated into an argument. As one child covered all the cars with his body so the pieces could not be seen or taken, the other child quickly snatched up all the puzzle cards. Stalemate. One controls the pieces and the other the cards. Now neither of them could play the game, and they both got mad. Being four and being human, these creative, verbal, competitive children were certainly not beyond using their hands instead of their words. However, they took time to look to me and the other parent across the room for arbitration and resolution. The other parent started to walk toward the quarreling boys to tell them that it's not nice to snatch things. I invited her to pause, and then I told the kids to *work it out*. I tried to convey in those three words all that I had been teaching them about sharing, taking turns, speaking with respect, letting it be okay to wait, using words to get what they want – *work it out* meant I had confidence in them and that I knew they were capable of solving the problem. Staying out of the fray is not easy, but it is effective when children have the tools to work with.

"Really? You are going to let us argue about this? How can we figure this out without a grown-up telling us who is right and who is wrong?" It was a perfect opportunity for these two kids to do just that – decide for themselves how to proceed. They did so quite amicably. As a parent, too often I want to resolve or fix things as quickly as possible. That choice may be expedient, but it doesn't help kids learn. Amazingly, these two kids truly negotiated and came up with a solution that was of their own making – much more satisfying than anything I could have forced upon them. And who wants to say or hear *NO* all day long? Isn't it better to direct attention to opportunities for learning and then encourage children to use their own capabilities to work through challenging moments?

Wise teachers can be wonderful traveling companions through transitions. As a teacher, I may observe a wide variety of needs in one class. For example, there may be a four-year-old who can actually hold a pencil and write her name; and there may be another child who hasn't developed that ability yet. The good teacher offers all children opportunities to hold many kinds of tools – crayons, paintbrushes, garden trowels – so that they can play and grow and explore at their level of development. Sometimes we get really bogged down in specific skills, especially ones that are school-related like *sit still, be quiet, pay attention, read this,* and *write that.* Children don't always operate with the same precision that the rules demand of them.

Most parents worry about their children making developmental milestones, mastering skills, being ready for school, and doing well in school. I remember being worried whether my child would "read on time." I looked up the issue in various pediatric books trying to find a definitive answer as to when my child should be able to read. My child loved for me to read to him each night, but he steadfastly refused to read to me even though he knew most of the words. He simply would not do it – either I read it to him or there was nothing. I asked, begged, teased and coddled, but he refused to read a word to me, nor did he want to read alone.

When I saw other kids in his Kindergarten class reading first grade chapter books, I spoke to the teacher. "Should my child be reading these big kid books too? What's wrong? I've read aloud to my child every single night without fail, since infancy." She said, "There is absolutely nothing wrong. Don't push the reading. Just enjoy it!" She suggested we make up alternate endings or introduce our own characters into the story, use stuffed animals to act out a story from a favorite book, use funny voices – essentially, just enjoy books and stories and being with my child at the end of the day. So I let up. I focused on enjoying bedtime books with my son, not trying to instruct him. Bedtime was much more pleasant, and soon he was reading those big kid chapter books on his own. I learned a valuable lesson in letting my child learn at his own pace. And in general, if I am uptight about something my kid is doing or not doing, I'm probably making him uptight too. Good grief, Mom! Reading should be fun!

We parents have an impulse to rescue our children. We want to "fix" them and their situation; we want to protect them. And we want to *make* them succeed. It is a hard lesson to learn that fixing them is not my role. My role, as a mom, is to love them, nurture them, and model the behaviors that I want to see in them. To be honest, I'm still working on this, and sometimes it is hard. If you want your child to read happily, then the first thing to do is read happily with your child and by yourself. If you want your child to hold a pencil and write, let them happily participate in preschool arts on their own terms – unidentifiable scribble scrabble pictures and ooey gooey projects that don't quite work are also included. I'm not saying that you don't lend help when needed. I have intervened on behalf of both of my children's schooling more than once. Each time I had empirical, classroom information that backed up the issues I was raising with a teacher or administrator. I made sure the educator knew I was interested in being their partner, not their critic. I know my children better than anyone else. I made sure that I had observed behaviors and asked questions of teachers about my child's behaviors and progress.

Sometimes it's hard to differentiate between letting your child learn through natural consequences and "helping" them see what they should do or how they should do it. Every family struggles to keep a balance. Does my child need a tutor? Is she really ready for kindergarten? All of these are good questions, sometimes easily answered and sometimes not. When it is unclear to me, I seek professional guidance. I begin with my pediatrician or a child specialist. I always listen to the "mommy voice" in the back of my mind. If something about my child's behavior concerns me, I tend to investigate it. At one point we sought speech therapy for our child, but only after lots of reading, talking with my husband, pediatrician and child specialists. I made sure that I understood his struggle. Only then did I come up with a plan to support him as he worked through his language transitions. Remember! You know your child better than anyone. This equips you to be the best judge of what is best for your child, especially when you remove your ambitions and fears and view your child clearly.

If your child is struggling through a transition – potty training, learning to be at school instead of home, learning to speak, teacher conflict – try to look at the behavior objectively and with a great deal of empathy. Get away from the thought of how annoying the behaviors may be to you. Take your own emotions and fears out of the equation. Though they may not change the way you would like, it is far better that they figure out their own strategy. Try to understand the child's frustration, and this may give you clues about how to support or redirect them so that they can be successful on their own. Lingering over goodbye upon arrival at school might give you warm fuzzies, but it might make your child's transition from home to school more difficult. So use carpool as the place where your child leaves you behind. Drop off quickly and confidently. Of course, give a kiss and grab a hug, but make sure you exude the confidence that your child is going to have a great time at school (despite those momentary tears first thing in the morning). I remember one Pre-K girl who cried and resisted getting out of the car every morning. Once in the classroom, she warmed up, participated and played and had a great day.

That said, getting her from the car to the classroom was tricky, so her brilliant mom devised an effective plan. She gave the child an envelope with my name on it and asked her to deliver it. Every morning I got a "special message via special delivery." I opened the envelope with a flourish and exclaimed something like her mom was hoping that we would go to the playground and collect pine cones today, and guess what, we are! After a week or so of envelopes, she walked into class with a spring in her step. Later, if I got an empty envelope, I recognized that she was having a rough morning and might need a little TLC. It was a simple but effective technique.

Sometimes a child's environment prevents him or her from managing a particular transition. If there are too many four-year-old kids in a small area, I can guarantee you there will be tears. If there is boisterous music playing and the air conditioner is thrumming and two children are making "music" with the pots and pans in the housekeeping center, it might not be reasonable to expect a child sensitive to sound to work on an art project. And it may appear strange, but sometimes it's hard for children to attend to things without movement. Perhaps they will listen and recall the story with more accuracy if they move about and act out the story. Children react differently to different environments. Especially as they get older, it is important for them to be self-aware and know what kinds of environments they prefer and why. This can affect simple things like doing homework or reading.

One teenager may need solitude and quiet. So he needs his own room with a desk full of office supplies. Another teenager can only focus with music and food. So he studies with ear buds in the kitchen close to the fridge.

As a preschool teacher, I learned to say funny things. All preschool teachers end up with their own lingo. Instead of saying "stop" or "walk" to a host of stampeding three-year-old kids in the hallway, I simply said, "Stop your feet, tell your feet to slow down." Or the perennial favorite, "Use your walking feet." If we were examining a bug on the playground, I might say, "Look with your eyes, not your hands." Somehow the very direct "stop your feet" would get their attention. Frequently, a child would pause in his dash in the hallway and actually look down at his feet like, "Huh, would you look at that, those are my feet." It's really hard to run and look at your feet at the same time. That pause was all that the child needed to remind him to slow it down. I also like phrases that suggest the children have direct and immediate control over themselves. I can only control my feet. And each child must learn to control his or hers. The same applies to the phrase I would use during circle time – "Put your eyes on me." Somehow "look at me" or "look up here" never worked. When I invited the children to put their eyes on me, some would actually touch the sides of their faces and roll their eyes towards me. They were acutely aware of their own eyes in their face and the act of turning them towards me. This is also helpful during circle time because if you are focused on your eyes and looking at whatever I'm doing, most likely your hands are not pulling your neighbor's hair and you probably aren't talking to another child. It would usually give me only ten seconds or less of complete attention of the group, but that's all I needed to give instructions and embark on an activity with a group of four-year-old children.

Sounds That Go Bump in the Night!

My child really didn't sleep through the night until elementary school. He gave up naps as a toddler and soon moved into a big bed because he could climb out of the crib – and climb over the gate in the doorway and be loose in the house in the middle of the night. I often woke up and heard noises downstairs; thinking burglars, I would find my two-year-old playing in the family room. We added locks up high on the doors because I was paranoid. I feared he would get out of the house while we were asleep. For my bouncing-baby-not-sleeping-through-the-night-boy, I placed snacks and water on his little table in his room. And together we picked out quiet toys for him to play with in the middle of the night. He had several nightlights to turn on instead of the overhead light. I encouraged him to play in his room rather than come into my room waking me up. He often woke me up to entertain him, tuck him back in bed or better yet, let him snuggle in mom and dad's bed. Eventually, I refused to let him get into our bed, so I got up and put him back in his own bed.

Still with regularity, he would try to sneak into my bed – I'd wake up and he would be curled up in a little ball like a puppy at the foot of the bed. Sometimes I'd wake up suddenly and he would be standing next to my bed, inches from my face, just watching me. Rarely was he upset or afraid; he was just AWAKE. I gave up on the concept of his sleeping through the night. I settled for his just staying in his own room. It seems as if we spent years getting him to stay in his room all night.

He was probably three years old when two nights running he tried several times to sneak into our bed and each time insisted that I get up and tuck him back in his bed. So, I said to my husband, "Okay, I'm going to be mean mommy tonight. I am NOT getting out of bed two or three times during the night, and he is not getting in bed with us." Sure enough, that night he got up and wanted me to tuck him in and I said, "Only once tonight, then I'm not getting out of my bed again." The second time he got up, I explained to him that I was not getting out of bed, that he had to take himself back to his bed. He stayed by my bedside – he stood there just watching me, waiting for me to fall back to sleep so he could sneak into my bed. Each time he started to climb into my bed, I roused myself up and stopped him. He got a bit frustrated with me. I told him, "You can sleep on the floor next to my bed but not in my bed." He curled up in a ball on the hardwood floor right next to me for one night only. The next night he came in, still woke me up, got a hug and kiss, and then he scampered back to his own room and his own bed. Whew! What an ordeal.

Listening for the Mommy Voice. . . from Home to School

The transition from home to school is a big deal for young children, as is changing the school experience – preschool to kindergarten to elementary school and then to middle school and high school – these are all equally huge transitions. Each of my children handled transitions differently, so that Mommy Voice once again helps in knowing the kind of environment where each child thrives versus the environments that bring on stress. When parents and teachers work together to encourage self-awareness, this helps children thrive and learn to navigate transitions. When parents observe how their child handles the school day, their observations and intuition can elicit wise decisions. For example, tuning in to whether the child finishes at one o'clock exhausted and then falls asleep in the car on the way home. Do they chatter about their day? Have they given up their afternoon nap? Do they eat well at school? How well do they play with other children? Do they experience different types of play and do they transition well from one type of play to another? Can the child run on the playground yelling about monsters or digging holes in the dirt and then transition to quiet time in the classroom reading a book? How well do they handle those daily transitions?

My child loved afternoon naps each day. I picked him up from kindergarten, and he fell asleep before we could pull out of carpool. During school he fell asleep during rest time, and the teacher would have to wake him up for the afternoon's activities. He also was ravenously hungry even though he had eaten lunch. I formed the habit of taking a lunchbox with snacks and drinks in afternoon carpool. By Christmas break his weariness and hunger were still the pattern – happy, pretty much coping with school, making friends, learning new things, but kind of stressed out, falling fast asleep during rest time and physically exhausted after school. So in January I had a conference with his teacher and I brought up the subject of repeating kindergarten. How can he learn what he needs to know if he isn't physically ready to handle a long day at school? Even today when he is almost a grown young man, he experiences his day intensely. I think he burns more calories sitting at the kitchen table doing homework than I do walking the dog. His experience of daily life is different from mine, but just as valid. When children are very young, parents need to make decisions about their daily life to keep them healthy and growing. But as children grow, these decisions need to shift from parent to child –

the child needs to be aware of his own needs and limitations and make good choices to care for himself daily.

Children need to tune in to their own needs and preferences as they learn to cope with school day demands. Whether a child needs lots of snacks or lots of physical activity, bringing awareness to these needs allows them to act accordingly. For example, at school my son left the lunchroom everyday to go to the bathroom just to wash his hands. He wasn't playing around; he just needed a break from all the noise in the cafeteria. He needed five or ten minutes of quiet. Luckily, he had a wise and understanding teacher. She let him go to the restroom each day, and he never got in trouble or stayed too long. He needed a short respite from the noise, and this helped him cope with the transitions he made the remainder of the day. He needed movement and he needed quiet – a walk across the school to the restroom took care of both needs.

The High School Years

Participation in church choir really helped with my child's transition from middle school to high school. Seeing familiar and friendly faces of other choir kids in the hallway the first week of high school was a big comfort in the midst of significant changes. It is quite an affirmation for a freshman to be greeted the first week of school by an upperclassman. The summer experiences at church – choir tours, mission trips and church retreats – have had powerful, lasting and wonderful effects on our teenagers. Teenagers need to have a place (other than home) where they belong, where they feel accepted. These experiences of stepping away from the regular routine in life seem to bring healthy perspectives and new connections.

The everyday drama of middle and high school can be a huge distraction and drain on energy for teenagers. You can't choose your teachers or who gets the locker next to you. But you can choose how you handle it. As a parent I keep having different versions of the same direction – stop thinking that you have been wronged or that things are unfair – think about the goal to achieve or the problem to solve, think about how to cope, avoid, prevent, or diffuse the stressful situation. It helps to stop, breathe and then explore more positive options. Don't behave in a way that makes a situation worse. Two seconds worth of anger and frustration and a poor reaction could gain a day of in-school suspension and ban you from field trips and parties. It's just not worth it. Days of consequences for a moment of trouble simply are not worth it. As you get older, the consequences can be dire and follow you for a long time.

My son had a high school teacher that he really didn't like. She was "difficult," she gave a lots of homework (really, huge assignments every night) and projects almost weekly. She was outgoing, strong, opinionated, a kind of in-your-face personality. Our child complained about the heavy load and I said, "Okay, I'll have a conference with your teacher and talk with her." At conference night, the teacher said, "Your son is one of my best students; he's doing great!" When I got home, I repeated this to my disbelieving son. I told him, "You show her that you take your school work seriously, you do your homework, it's complete and on time, you don't talk in class and she thinks everything is fine." I explained to my son that he was in her class to learn biology, not to like her. "You don't really need to like her or her assignments, but you do need to pass biology. She doesn't control your grade; you do."

Various transitions require teachers and parents to be patient and trust the children to make good choices. Neither can make the transitions for them. Children must learn and live through it, whatever it is. Whether it's potty training or learning how to make friends in middle school, parents need to look for ways that they can support, nurture, redirect behavior in a positive direction. I can force my kids to get their homework finished, but I can't force them to get along with their peers. I ensure that they have opportunities to be with their peers and then calmly listen when they are upset about an event. Transitions are by nature a process, and it is okay if these transitions are not clear-cut and precise. What works for one child might not for another.

Well, this is my story, the story of a mother and teacher, about my own transitions as a parent and stories that illustrate the various transitions that children make on their way to maturity.

9. Learning to Live with Bad News

"In ways that I cannot explain, this loss has become a gift to me, a gift that will enable me to journey the path of not knowing in hopeful, loving and caring ways."

Some days are loaded heavier than others. Such a day came to me in May, 2014 as my wife and I were vacationing at a Georgia beach. In the quiet following breakfast my cell phone rang. I answered and the man at the other end identified himself as a missing persons detective in Omaha, Nebraska. Since the disappearance of our son in January, he had been searching for him, so I had spoken with this detective on the phone many times.

After a brief greeting, there was a long pause. Then he said, "I have some information for you about your son; we found his body in Illinois." With those words came dead silence for what seemed like half an hour. I felt a searing pain rising inside me. My breath deepened as it mingled with the tears running down my face. The detective continued, "His body has been found in Illinois at a train yard. It appears that a car filled with coal was dumped on him, and his body was so mangled that it had become unrecognizable."

He continued to explain that a positive identification had been made through information from his dental records. Since his disappearance on January 29, we had waited desperately for some word. Here it was the thirteenth day of May, and this was the first knowledge we had since he turned up missing.

While both my brain and my heart were processing this announcement, I remember experiencing a long silence while I was getting control of my emotions. After the silence, I began asking questions about where the body was, what they thought had happened, and why it took so long to discover his body. I wondered if he had suffered greatly during that period when he was missing. I had no idea what to do next. I recognized that I had to retrieve his body and plan for a memorial service of his life. The detective had shared all the information he had and could do nothing more. My wife, my daughter and I grieved, and we found strength and encouragement in each other.

The Mortician

Although much of what follows is still hazy, I do recall speaking with a mortuary in Illinois. That conversation reminded me of all the times I had been to the mortuary with parishioners who had lost a loved one; never before had I been in the place of choosing and planning how to commemorate a son's life. So much comes to mind from the conversation that I had with the mortician. Early on, he began to go over the charges for his services. He estimated the cost to be approximately $2,700 for the cremation and an additional $250 for a box to transfer the body for the cremation.

Quite frankly, I was stunned! I explained to this man the circumstances of our son's death. I informed him that we did not have unlimited resources. Then I asked him if there was anything he could do about the exorbitant charges. I told him that mortuaries I knew of charged far less for a cremation and that his charges seemed excessive. He agreed to check with the owner of the mortuary and get back to me. Later in the day he called back and agreed to reduce the charges to $1,400. I was struck by the fact that so many people in times of grief do not have the presence of mind to deal responsibly with all the issues precipitated by the death of a family member.

Struggling with difficult financial decisions in a time of grief reminded me of the people I have guided in an Alzheimer's support group each week. In this group I have repeatedly noted that people are required to make some of the biggest decisions of their lives at the most emotionally charged moments of their lives. When we are grieving, we are more vulnerable and less able to handle our life effectively.

Facing Reality

When the conversation with the detective ended and I hung up the phone, my wife and I began talking about our feelings surrounding the confirmation of our son's death. As I tried to give voice to what was going on inside my soul, I realized that I had no words to express my feelings; I was wordless, something I seldom experience. The words of Scripture came to me from Paul's writing where he describes how the Holy Spirit gives voice to and expresses for us groans that are too deep for words (Romans 8:26). At that moment I understood what Paul was writing about. I knew that I had no words to pray the prayer of my heart; I had no ability to speak my prayers; I was stuck in the pain of inexpressible loss. At this time I was so deeply comforted by my wife's presence. Neither of us had words, but we had a feeling of togetherness with each other. We were filled with memories of our lives together as a family.

Our Son's Last Days

This son had suffered with both mental illness and addiction for most of his life. He had been to scores of treatment centers, seeking deliverance from these demons within. In the final days of his life he had spent six months in jail. When he got out of jail, he went into Oxford House, a halfway house in Omaha to help addicted persons. He spent only a couple of days there; he began to hear voices, have delusions and hallucinations, and I believe these psychotic symptoms frightened the residents of Oxford House. He was asked to leave that place of refuge in the middle of the night. He complied; he threw all of his belongings into his car and left. As he was leaving, he called me and when I learned of his circumstances, I made arrangements for him to go to a motel for the next week. During the days that followed we sought to find a place for him to receive the care that he needed.

He went to another facility in Omaha, the Bridges of Hope. This hospital cares for people with both mental illness and addiction. For reasons that I do not understand, he was turned away; it still troubles me that they did not accept him into this treatment facility. I learned later that he left the center and drove from Omaha toward Lincoln, Nebraska. On his trip from Omaha to Lincoln, he had a flat tire, abandoned his car and began walking down the highway. The temperature had dipped to 5 or 10 degrees below zero. Fortunately, he was picked up by a state policeman who took him to a facility in Lincoln. He only spent one night in that facility and the next morning walked out early. That day was January 29. From that day until May 13 we had heard nothing from him until the missing persons detective called us.

We can only imagine what went on during those 105 days. So many possibilities crossed our minds. Had he been kidnapped? Had some ill-fated event destroyed his life? Had he been murdered? Was he lost? I have wondered if he hopped a freight train and rode it from Omaha to the banks of the Mississippi River in Illinois. All I know is that his body was found at a place by the Mississippi River where coal was dumped from one container into another.

I had made a deposit to his bank account about the time that he got out of jail, and that money had not been touched. So many unanswered questions remained. Furthermore, I had feared he was dead because he never went more than two days without calling either me or his mother. Even when he was in jail, he spoke with me on the phone. He often called to ask me if I had time to do daily devotions with him. We frequently read together the daily devotion used by Alcoholics Anonymous. After reading a devotion, we reflected on what the particular reading stirred in our individual lives. This son in his searching enriched my connection with God as he enriched so many other aspects of my life. Jesus spoke about encountering the Spirit of God among the least of our brothers and sisters. Certainly, those who suffer from mental illness and addiction are counted among the least.

Dispensing with the Shame

So much shame surrounds mental illness and addiction because in our culture we are encouraged to keep these illnesses a secret. These blemishes must be kept secret because people who suffer with them are often judged to be defective and should be ashamed of their state. Addicted people are very much like the lepers in the days of Jesus. They were commanded to walk around the community ringing bells and shouting "unclean, unclean." Their crying out meant "stay away from me." Paradoxically, some of the people who suffer from these diseases have a depth of appreciation for life that goes far beyond what many others feel or acknowledge.

The following days and weeks have been filled with waves of grief mixed with wonderful memories of the experiences we shared. Together with my wife and daughter, we began planning a memorial service to be held in Atlanta. Prior to that service, our son's girlfriend, the mother of our granddaughter, had a beautiful service in Omaha celebrating the life of her daughter's father. My wife chose to wait for the service in Atlanta, and my daughter and I flew to Omaha to also attend the service there.

Our two children were very close through all the years as they were growing up. It was healing for my daughter and me to have individual time with each other on the plane to Omaha. We shared many memories of family vacations, Christmas gatherings, and birthdays. These memories flooded my mind and took me back to more pleasant days. One particular memory emerged from the summer when my two children and I rode bicycles from Atlanta to Savannah, Georgia. We participated in an outing called Bicycle Ride Across Georgia. What a great experience that was for the three of us.

Memorial in Omaha

When we arrived at the airport in Omaha, my pain surfaced again. As I walked into the airport, I remembered the last time I was there, and how my son ran down the concourse and greeted me and my daughter. That experience reminded me of the power of place and the richness of memory, and how they come alive again when we revisit them.

When my daughter and I arrived, we picked up the rental car and drove to his girlfriend's house. After a brief visit with her and our granddaughter, we headed to the place where the memorial service was to be held. From a distance we looked up at a most beautiful chapel, the Holy Family Shrine in Omaha. The Chapel is constructed almost totally of glass and sits atop a high hill. His girlfriend and her family are Roman Catholic, and this enabled us to have the service in this beautiful chapel. Because of the rules of the church, the priest was not able to lead the prayer service because our son was not Roman Catholic. However, we were allowed to request a Presbyterian minister to lead the service in this Catholic chapel. She was a former Roman Catholic who had converted to become a Presbyterian minister. She also happened to be a practicing Jungian analyst. I found her very open to leading the service in a way that would be both caring and significant to all concerned.

A special part of the service was when our eight-year-old granddaughter spoke a few words about her father. I remember how she confidently walked down the aisle, took her place at the front of the chapel, and began the service by talking about her daddy. Her words amazingly depicted his love for her and her love for him. I will always treasure the memories of sitting in that sacred place experiencing their love for our son. The service was a beautiful recognition of his life and what his life had meant to them.

The beauty of that place combined powerfully with the inspired words spoken by the minister. She was able to acknowledge the devastating nature of our son's illness and give voice to the reality of his delusions, hallucinations and his addiction. In turn, she also spoke of the beauty of his spirit and emphasized the beauty that he created with his artistic gifts. She spoke of the magnificent landscaping that he did and the attractive plans that he developed. She spoke also of the deep way in which he loved his daughter and cared for her. I was so deeply grateful for the way in which she emphasized who he was in the depth of his soul.

Both as a minister and mental health professional, this pastor knew so well that those who suffer from addiction are not defined by their illness. She made it clear that he was defined by his soul, emphasizing that he is a child of God. I have prayed that his life might show addicted people that they are not defined by their illness. We often had talked about how counterproductive it was to keep as a secret the suffering of persons with mental illness. We both were conscious of how secrecy causes people to suffer in isolation, and isolation contributes to the depth of the problem. We are immersed in a culture that values privacy to such an extent that it is detrimental to the whole community. As Christians, our faith is sustained, supported and informed by our connection with a believing community.

The Unexpected Transition

This death created a major life transition for me and our family. Everything will be different from this point forward. Because of our son's struggles and our love for him, we had spent unbounded time and energy caring for him and walking with him through the dark places in his life. His death creates a void. Since so much of my life has been structured around caring for him, now what? What will I do without this focus? As I move into my future, restructuring my life will be a major issue. I have begun to ask myself how I will utilize the time, energy and learning gained from this caring. How can I utilize it to be helpful to others?

Today I have a painful void and feel an emptiness that nothing at this moment fills. This struggle makes me keenly aware that I do not know what will happen next, nor do I know what I will do next. However, I feel mysteriously open to whatever comes.

Dealing with this void has brought me into a place of not knowing. I feel like the great prophet Abraham who "went out not knowing." I am driven to be responsive to the present moment. I want to be cautiously observant of life's unfolding. In the past I have been blind to what was really happening in the moment. This failure springs not only from unawareness but also from entertaining predetermined and fixed ideas of what I should be and how I ought to feel. Being willing to walk the way of unknowing makes it easier to process the raw data of my everyday life.

Over the years I have observed many people who have gotten stuck in major life transitions. Sometimes their disillusionment, anger and sense of loss have closed them to reality. Without a constant watchfulness, we can easily become bitter, resistant and stuck in old habits so that we are unable to live or to love. Wholesome people have repeatedly demonstrated that forgiveness is one of the most important qualities of a well-lived life. If we are unable to forgive our anger at others or towards God, it will block the creative unfolding of our lives. Without forgiveness we will be slaves to resentment.

I cannot explain why this loss has opened me to the deeper realities of my life, rather than closing me through resentment; I feel no resentment for all that has happened to me. In ways that I cannot explain, this loss has become a gift to me, a gift that will enable me to journey the path of not knowing in hopeful, loving and caring ways.

As I sort through my thoughts, feelings, and yearnings, I realize that we all experience loss differently. My wife, for example, processes life in different ways from me. She is an artist. A few days ago I came home from counseling to find her standing at her easel painting a portrait of our son. Painting a beautiful portrait offers her a way to express the depth of her love. She was very close to our son throughout his life. She spent many hours visiting with him, caring for him, and searching for educational and mental health placements for him. He was a handsome young man, and as I observed her standing at her easel painting his portrait, I realized that painting him was her way of continuing to remember and love him. She feels the pain and agony as well as the beauty and strength of his soul, all very much a part of his life. As she paints, she is remembering his strong and good qualities – like his blue eyes and blond hair, his joyful spirit and compassionate heart. Gazing at the portrait, we have both laughed and cried as memories surfaced. Standing there together, we reviewed different segments of his thirty-seven years. I appreciate the ways she and I differently engage life and its losses, and I rejoice in knowing we are complementary to each other.

Our daughter was very close to her brother. They were good friends and shared many fun experiences together. As our son went through some of his spells, his sister sometimes felt frightened by his psychotic episodes and use of drugs. I understand her responses because his illnesses created enormous personality changes and mood swings, often in unpredictable and alarming ways. She dealt with his death by working diligently to plan his memorial service in Atlanta. She worked with the music, the hymns and the order of his service along with having strong ideas about a reception to follow the memorial service. She is full of energy and life, and she has focused some of her grief into the recognition of her brother. In other aspects of life, she deals with transitions and losses by working harder and finding ways to channel her thoughts and energy. For example, for several years she has participated in triathlons; her running, swimming and biking help her process feelings of fear, loss and grief.

A Prayer for Our Son
Almighty, Gracious, and Ever Present God,
> *Where can we go from your Spirit? Or where can we flee from your presence?*
>> *If we ascend into heaven, you are there;*
>> *If we make our beds in hell, behold, you are there.*
>> *If we should take the wings of the morning,*
>> *And dwell in the uttermost parts of the sea,*
>> *Even there your hand shall lead us,*
>> *And your right hand shall hold us.*
>> *If we say, "Surely the darkness shall cover us,"*
>> *Even the night shall be light about us;*

Even the darkness shall not hide us from you,
Because the night shines as the day;
The darkness and the light are both alike to you.
You have laid your hand upon us.

* * *

Thanks be to you, Oh God! That ...
Wherever we go, there you are!
Whatever we face, there you are!
In the midst of our fear and doubt, there you are!
Even in our deep loneliness and staggering sense of loss,
there you are also!

Assured of your persistent love, your compassionate care and enduring mercy, we look to you today:

Hear our thanksgiving for our son and for his life, for the loving contributions he made to others.

Be with our friends. May your Presence sustain them, may your love enfold them and hold each one close to your heart.

Through your unceasing graciousness, our son is with you. You have received him. You have delivered him from confusion and pain and he is becoming all that you intend him to be.

Thanks be to you, O God, for Christ – for his life, his death and his awesome resurrection that gives substance to our faith and nourishes our hope.

We pray not only for this family in their time of grief, but for all of us who are passing this way, that we may be strong in faith, fruitful in hope and radiant in Spirit as we face our own transition into that deeper dimension of your Presence.

As we all make our journey home, may this prayer be in each of our hearts . . .

God be the love to search and keep me,
God be the prayer to have my voice,
God be the strength to now uphold me,
O Christ, surround me! O Christ, surround me! Amen

10. The Paradox of Waiting

"I was strangely at peace even though my life hadn't changed on the outside."

I'm impatient, and I am very used to effecting change in my life. I haven't always had things exactly the way I wanted them, but I always felt capable of making a move. I felt competent at maneuvering and arranging things in my life so that I might be happier.

This began to shift when I was around forty. I was married with two young girls and after several years of marriage, my husband and I were estranged. I lived in the guest room, having become more or less skillful at avoiding the inevitable hostility which arose if we were in the same space for more than a moment. The girls had become used to the tension as it was all they knew at home. I lived as a recluse, taking my evening mug of chai tea into my room after they were in bed and reading books about enlightenment. Marital counseling was a failure. I was up against a thick solid brick wall. The marriage was dead.

I had given up on almost all relationships with anyone except my children. However, divorce seemed impossible. I couldn't imagine working full time, becoming financially insecure, and turning my kids' lives upside down; nor could I bear the idea of shared custody. Being away from my children, even if it was only for a couple of days a week, was not an option at their tender age. I calculated that my best move was to wait long enough for my girls to become more independent; then I could move out and start my life as a single mom.

Filled with hostility, I waited a couple of years in emotional solitude as the mystics (from all religious traditions) kept me company at night. Then it hit me one day – my waiting wasn't really waiting at all; it was just another strategy I was using to get my way. And it wasn't working well. I was miserable. For the first time I realized I was at the end of my rope. God had me pinned down; it was checkmate. I couldn't make one more move. The only thing left was to give up – for real.

I prayed, not to any notion of an intervening God who would change my circumstance, but I just prayed in a last ditch effort to give up control of myself and my life. I remember the feeling that came the night I prayed for the first time. It didn't matter that no one was listening; it was just a big relief, after giving up, not to be in charge anymore. Having admitted that I was completely powerless to change myself, I felt relaxed in a way I hadn't ever experienced.

That night my true waiting began, as I let go of waiting as a way of being in charge. I felt softer and more open after I stopped strategizing. I was strangely at peace even though my life hadn't changed on the outside. I think I was able to wait because I had the feeling that the Universe was waiting for me. I knew Love was waiting very quietly.

After a short time, the man who would become the Love of my life did indeed appear very quietly, though not as anything but a friend at first. I can't help but ponder the synchronicity of Love appearing out of simple waiting.

Was this a transition? You bet!

11. My Life on the Big Screen

"Thanks to my Shadow,
each transformation,
birthed from
faithfulness
in uncertainty
and unknowing,
liberates me
time and time again
into gratefulness—
leaving me happily consumed
in muted wonder."

For years I have been drawn into (what little I can understand) the writings of Stephen Hawking. I stayed up nights delving into Hawking's *A Brief History of Time*. His exploration and discoveries relating to black holes intrigued me to no end. His impassioned choice to live into his highest potential and to work with unchosen, unwanted, and monumental circumstances is more than astonishing. While attending Cambridge in the 1960s, he was diagnosed with a debilitating disease and given two years to live. He called forth his innate capacities to defy probable and inevitable predictions of demise, and he found the courage to resurrect those hidden inner forces. To this day, he is very much alive, though a false report of his death appeared on Facebook in 2014.

I found myself weeping as I watched the previews of *The Theory of Everything*, the film portraying his life. If the film is anything close to the previews, it will touch the psychic depths of our generation and deliver a well-deserved Oscar.

This man's life is worthy of reflection, and his contribution to my life and many others stays with me as I give my memory free rein. My memory banks are bristling and enlivened!! I am at once taken back in time to my boyhood when my dad was the manager of the only movie theater in Ayden, our eastern North Carolina village of 1000, where I was born (and lived in the same house until I was married). This little post-Depression, pre-war southern village was getting off the ground, thriving economically in the middle of countless tobacco farms. The "Show" was THE entertainment center of our town, jam-packed every weekend, and it was located two blocks from my home. The emotional energy influenced by movies was palpable. The collective influence of many movies at that time excelled any technological device available today. I vividly recall the trance-like feeling of seeing *Bambi* in Technicolor! At times, all was euphoric in that southern *"Pleasantville"* —as far as I knew.

Gone with the Wind came out in 1939 when I was five years of age; I felt so proud to see my dad standing on the stage before the show started, personally speaking to a packed house. Movies became my open window out into a wider world. I watched countless movies two or three times a day, memorizing and quoting certain phrases, from the time I was five until I "graduated" from my various jobs at the theater. I sold my first bag of popcorn to a customer when I was in the third grade; the kind black gentleman gave me a dollar and I gave him $1.65 in change, for a ten-cent bag of popcorn. He quietly walked over to the ticket booth and talked to my dad about something. My dad came over to me and said, "Sonny boy, you can bring me the money from now on, and I will help you make change, okay?"

I worked at the picture show during WWII, watching my dad divvy out gas rationing stamps and sell war bonds. My mind was riveted by the gruesome Hitler-dominated war pictures on "Time Marches On," the regular newsreel updates. My identity in that small community hinged on my being the oldest son of the manager of the local theater. By the time I was in the eighth grade I got up the courage to tell my mother that I wanted to stop working with Daddy, and she knew that it would be quite a challenge for my dad to get this news. "You go tell your father," she encouraged me. It took a few days, but I got up the courage to say the words. Indeed, it was a traumatic paradigm shift to bravely announce to my dad, sitting in a rocking chair on the front porch, that I was going to work elsewhere. He silently sulked, feeling abandoned by his oldest son. I "broke away" and got a job washing cars at a filling station; then I worked at the local hardware store. These were huge decisions for an eighth grader, believe me!

I find myself making a nostalgic, spontaneous association back into those post-Depression, pre-war, war-time and post-war years in the South. While I am "there" in my mind, sitting here now I must say that I grew up in what I now realize was a pitifully unconscious, "Christianized" racist bubble, and working at the "show" slowly helped unravel and awaken my naivety. Our black brothers and sisters at that time sat upstairs on wooden seats in the balcony; whites sat below in the cushioned seats. I felt an overwhelming sense of unfairness that "they" did not have restrooms; they would come downstairs to literally beg (holding themselves in agony) my dad for permission to run out behind the building to go to the bathroom. Feelings of injustice and unfairness coiled up inside my confused heart. An encounter with Deecie, our beloved black maid, finally split me open when she took a switch to my white behind and said, "Hal Junior, don't you ever again call me a n-----, you hear that!!? I's a person just like you!!"

I didn't know until years later how that backyard encounter exploded something inside my little head. I was thoroughly brainwashed, and I somehow realized I had a choice—to remain locked into prejudice—or begin to deal with my own stuff. It was the beginning of a radical change, and I now look back and see how that became my own personal "road less traveled" as a southern white boy. That woman, God bless dear Deecie, loved me, and she ushered me out of that limited southern culture mindset when she uttered those powerful and true words.

I think because of that early boyhood encounter with Deecie, I later found myself drawn to sit upstairs in that tiny hometown theater, alone among my black "family." I felt something healing deep in my soul before I could even begin to put conscious words around it. Something far deeper and beyond any rational thinking drew me upstairs time and time again. I never told any white person about this. When Daddy found me upstairs, he would gently touch my shoulder and tell me it was time to go home.

These are happy and grateful tears I feel when I think of my *Gone with the Wind* years, and they are tears energized by the nudges offered by this new movie, *The Theory of Everything*, depicting the extraordinary life of Stephen Hawking. This man's dedication to find and follow his life mission reminds me of a greater and more important world that continues to evolve and challenge us into that mystical Oneness where *"...all things belong."* (1 Cor. 3:21)

WITHOUT MY SHADOW

Without my Shadow,
blinded and unaware of
sheer dynamic forces
between opposites,
I would remain
desperately dangerous
and innocently oblivious,
unable to receive and transmute
life's impending circumstances
designed to transform
fear into love,
projections into insight,
blame into responsiveness,
judgments into opportunities.
Without my Shadow,
I would miss the
continuity and magic
of the present moment.
I would be
left on my own,
lost and unaware,
meandering through my past,
trifling naively into the future.
Thanks to my Shadow,
choices and consequences
divine their impartial
and judicious outcomes
with precision.

Her dark Refining Wheel
grinds away
all the dross,
and all the loss,
until each obscure shade
kneels triumphantly
into the wonder
and wisdom
of destiny.
Thanks to my Shadow,
each transformation,
birthed from
faithfulness
in uncertainty
and unknowing,
liberates me
time and time again
into gratefulness—
leaving me happily consumed
in muted wonder.

12. My Son Is Gay

"When we know one another as we truly are, both warts and giftedness, and still love and cherish each other, we experience the love we all desire."

My story begins on a gentle summer evening, our date night. Our son, a soon-to-be high school senior, was in Germany as an exchange student. Our soon-to-be sophomore daughter was on an outing with our church youth group. We'd spent the afternoon at a beach and were having dinner recounting some of the blessings in our family, especially our two teenagers. I said, "But I have one fear." My husband looked at me and asked, "Do you think our son is gay?" Totally shocked that he had a similar thought, I was only able to nod. Whatever words we used to describe our intuitive concern, we agreed we needed to talk with him.

When Zach returned from Germany, we sat down with him for "the talk." We explained how we had conferred with each other about our joint concern, and how we had wondered if he had questions about his male identity. We promised that nothing he answered could ever affect our love for him. We suggested counseling if he had questions. He listened without comment or reaction. He simply answered, "I'll get back to you about that." Whether by God's grace or our son's wisdom, we got extra time to adjust to this new possibility in our lives.

Soon after Christmas that year, he came to us saying he wanted to have "the talk." We thought we were ready for any eventuality, but having him confirm that he indeed considered himself to be gay was difficult. We asked why he had delayed in telling us. Did he think we'd refuse to believe him or disown him? He pointed out that many gays are rejected by their families. He thought it would be easier for us if he waited until he was away at college to speak about his identity. He had always been a thoughtful child, mature beyond his years. We did not know before that conversation that he had already ventured out to several events for gay teens in the greater metropolitan area where we lived. In that setting he had heard some pretty sad stories about parental rejection. He explained that he was telling us about himself now because he wanted to be "out" with his high school friends. We reassured him again that nothing would change our love for him. We got his permission to ask him all kinds of questions. We didn't want him to sense any lack of support or love, but we did need to understand him and help him be certain before going public.

Over the next weeks we asked a lot of questions. Did he want counseling? No, he didn't believe that was necessary. He was sure of who he was. He had always known he was different. When sexuality was discussed in a fifth- grade science class, he had wondered even then if being gay was what made him feel different. We asked if there had ever been any abuse, sexual or otherwise, and he said that there had not been any. He answered all our questions calmly and respectfully as we felt our way toward a clearer understanding. Through all our children's lives, we had developed a way of being with them that encouraged openness and honest discussion. We didn't put the tough stuff under the table. We had talked openly with them about our own mid-life career changes as we were making them. I'm thankful we had this history and pattern of relating. It made this conversation easier.

Unfortunately, we don't recognize assumptions until they're challenged. As a mom, I began to realize the assumptions I had that were not going to be realized. I began to feel the losses that I would suffer. My family table would never include another daughter and several little Zachs playing in my yard, laughing with grannie. As an only child I had longed for a big family – a Norman Rockwell-type picture. No wedding! No chance to be mother of the best groom in the world!

But even worse were the fears that I had for my son. He wasn't the shy, retiring type. He was intelligent, well spoken privately and publicly. Would friends or their parents reject him? I wondered about all the ways he could possibly be hurt. Would he be assaulted by someone who could not accept his being gay? What would happen to him when he attended college? What about AIDS? These questions plagued me over twenty years ago when there wasn't the acceptance we know now. Matthew Shepard's terrible death in Wyoming at the hands of brutes had not yet awakened the public to the very real dangers of being honest about one's identity. At first, the fears were overwhelming.

A most important thing to be learned from our story is the value of honest communication. Facing into the questions, tears, anxieties and issues together is essential. It's the first work of any transition, and it can deepen relationships. When we know one another as we truly are, both warts and giftedness, and still love and cherish each other, we experience the love we all desire.

I didn't consider it then, but the fact that I was a Christian pastor may have played a part in our son's fear of rejection. I realized the real reason that he had refused to participate in the church's youth group. It wasn't because the only teens there were from the local high school, which he didn't attend. He obviously knew from the youth pastor what Christians thought of homosexuality. This pastor had made it clear that homosexuality was a sin. Many people in my mainline denomination were beginning to question the traditional interpretations of scripture around homosexuality, but not this particular pastor.

What occurred then, I now recognize usually happens. When our son came out of the closet, we went into the closet. We needed time to adjust. Among the parents of our son's friends, only one called me. She was kind and caring. She was disappointed that her daughter's best friend was no longer boyfriend material, but she said they had always loved Zach and still did. My husband and I remained closeted, talking only with the couples in a small group we attended. This group had already been through many testing experiences together, and they heard us in a caring and accepting way. They didn't try to fix us. They promised to stand by Zach and by us. They lived this promise through the years that followed.

The church community and my pastoral position presented my next hurdle. Would members of the congregation and the other pastors judge my husband and me – that we had somehow failed to properly raise our son? Would I be rejected and not deemed a good Christian because I had a gay son and supported him? Fear distorted both my vision and, I suspected, theirs.

I was closeted in agony. I loved and accepted my son and would support him no matter what it cost. After five years of seminary and internships which I began at mid-life, I had been called to a pastoral position by a congregation in our community. I loved ministry. It was going well. My life had meaning and purpose. Was I going to lose all this? What was the head of staff's position on ordination of gays? I feared that the response of the church would "eat me up." The role of gays was becoming a "hot topic" in numerous Christian communities, and I didn't want to become a "one message" pastor. I wrestled with conflicting emotions and with God's will in my prayers.

Finally, I told the head of staff our story and offered my resignation. He refused my resignation and wanted to know if anyone, staff or members, disparaged me. His response was another sign of God's grace. He gave me the space and safety I needed to study scripture and determine my response to the interpretations of scripture that had surrounded me in seminary.

I entered into this study with two solid thoughts. First, God loves our son just as God loves our daughter and all of us. Secondly, *I knew that for gay persons being homosexual was not a choice.* My intellect understood this and my mother's heart knew it, although it was different from what I had been taught. Just as I never chose to be heterosexual, our son never chose to be homosexual. It was who he was. These thoughts were important in my transition because if Zach was created this way, how could God /Jesus reject him if he lived the truth of who he was. Today I still hear people say, "Love the sinner but not the sin." That doesn't work. Sexuality is core to a person's identity whether heterosexual or homosexual. A gay person and their sexuality cannot be separated, so this phrase amounts to hurtful rejection.

Today there are many resources for the study and interpretation of what scripture says and doesn't say about homosexuality. They are much better and more thorough than anything I could write here, but three insights were helpful in my theological transition.

First, context is always important in interpretation and never more so than in Romans 1. Paul is attempting to connect with a community of believers who do not know him personally. He is describing the situation in which they lived and a culture against which they stood. They lived at the epicenter of a society "filled with every kind of wickedness" (*Rom.1:29*). Rome, the Empire's capital, was a culture filled with wealth and power seekers whose prestige was increased by self-indulgent excess and sexual license. (Read Eugene Peterson's paraphrase of Romans 1:26-32 in *The Message* to catch the flavor of a culture that was "all lust and not love.") Neither Paul nor the culture he is describing had knowledge of committed, monogamous, same-gender relationships. He had no understanding, as we do, of the tie between identity and sexual orientation. I concluded that Paul and other New Testament texts cannot be applied literally to same gender committed relationships which struggle just as heterosexual couples do to live the kind of love described by Paul in 1 Corinthians 13.

Second, Jesus never addressed the topic of homosexuality. But he always went to the outsider: the excluded woman at the well, the lepers, the beggars, the blind and deaf. Until recently, who was totally excluded from the church and from much of society but the homosexual? Have you ever ministered to a man who knew he was homosexual, but married a female because he feared exclusion from church and family? Have you ever ministered to someone who decided he could no longer live a lie even if it meant losing family? I have, and I have seen the distress and destruction that these attempts to conform cause. Jesus would not desire this destructiveness. *He would be with the outcasts.*

Third, I discovered Isaiah 56:4-7, not a text often mentioned in the debate. In Israel eunuchs were considered sexually deformed and therefore excluded from Temple worship. Through Isaiah God says,

> "To the eunuchs who keep my Sabbaths, who choose what pleases me and hold fast to my covenant – to them I will give within my temple and its walls a memorial and a name better than sons and daughters; I will give them an everlasting name that will not be cut off. And foreigners who bind themselves to the LORD to serve him, to love the name of the LORD, and to worship him, all who keep the Sabbath without desecrating it and who hold fast to my covenant – these I will bring to my holy mountain and give them joy in my house of prayer. Their burnt offerings and sacrifices will be accepted on my altar; for my house will be called a house of prayer for all nations."

I wonder if the Ethiopian eunuch described in Acts 8, who came to Jerusalem on pilgrimage, was reading not only Isaiah 53 but also chapter 56. Here is someone whose sexuality was not religiously acceptable. He was excluded from Temple worship. Yet Philip was led by the Holy Spirit to join him in his chariot. He reached out to the outcast and explained Jesus' message of liberation, love and acceptance. The eunuch, just like the woman at the well, wanted Jesus' life-giving water. The outsider was baptized and became part of the community of believers; he was accepted as he was. While these are not verses explicitly about homosexuality, they do show inclusion of a person who was deemed sexually impure.

I began tentatively to express my views within the church staff and among close friends who knew "our secret." I realized I was biased. No interpreter begins from a neutral perspective as much as it is desired or claimed. Our experiences color what we hear, see and feel. In my conversations, I owned the experience that colored what I understood in scripture. Because of this new understanding and also because I didn't want to become identified as a "single issue pastor," I didn't become a crusader for change in the church's position.

In quieter ways I began to take action. I encouraged the staff to refer parents to me who were facing the same questions. I also discovered parents who were trying to reconnect with children previously rejected. I met one couple who wanted me to "fix" or find someone to "fix" their son. I couldn't change their mind, and my heart wept. I also met with the youth pastor and asked him to include me in discussions with teens and their parents around the issue of homosexuality. Another parent and I formed a support group, "Christian Parents of Gays and Lesbians." (I had explored Parents and Friends of Lesbians and Gays {PFLAG} but concluded that it was too political for us at this early stage of transition.) We publicized our group to churches in our area; a few parents came. We provided resources and support, but without an activist agenda. I still get calls and emails from parents who are facing the question of their child's sexuality. Discovering that your child is gay continues to raise questions and requires adjustment.

Our son and daughter had the usual childhood skirmishes, but loved each other deeply and still do. We asked Zach to talk with his sister directly when he was coming out because it was his news to tell, not ours. There was never a question in her mind about her support for her brother. There was, however, the problem of the youth group.

She had many friends there and seemed to navigate the waters of controversy without distress. When "Youth Sunday" rolled around, the youth led worship, including the morning sermon. Zach's sister was asked to be one of the speakers.

We had always encouraged our children's independence, asked their views and respected their opinions. I chose not to ask any questions about her topic or talk. I hadn't realized what a gifted speaker she was. She had the congregation laughing as she talked about her faith, but then she turned to her "one problem." She picked up the Bible and read Romans 1:24-27. She then described her brother's sterling qualities and ended by saying, "He is gay." She looked directly at the congregation and said, "I don't know what I'm going to do with this scripture, but I love my brother and so does God." We were no longer hiding! People who knew us well already knew our story. But now we were "outted" to the whole congregation. My husband and I were very proud of our daughter. *Her brother was away at college, but had given his approval to her plan.*

My final pastoral transition came when I helped lead a workshop on the issues surrounding the ordination of homosexuals. Another pastor laid out the scriptural interpretations and arguments on both sides of the issue. Then I told our family's story and explained why I saw no reason that a Christian church could not ordain a gay pastor, elder or deacon as long as they met the congregation's call criteria – to be of sound faith, having good character, trying to live their faith. I have become an advocate for same-gender marriage. We must call our gay sisters and brothers to committed, covenanted relationships. I am grateful that the church I serve has also made this transition.

Along with these pastoral transitions, I was continuing my motherly transition. Several marker points may be important, especially for those who are making this journey. Christmas of Zach's freshman year in college, all four of us were in the kitchen preparing, cooking and talking. I can't recall what I said in response to someone's comment, but suddenly there was silence. I mean dead silence. I looked up from what I was chopping and the three of them were all looking at me. Our daughter grinned, "Mom just made a funny." Since I'm a terrible joke-teller, when I actually get a punch line right or offer some funny quip, it's usually noticed. Our daughter said again, "Mom just made a funny about homosexuality." My family laughed and hugged. As Anne LaMott says, "When the laughter comes, you know grace has fallen."

Another milestone was hearing about Zach's college boyfriend and then inviting him to join us on a family ski trip. No matter how much you support your son, seeing him hold hands with another male the first time is hard. And the first kiss is even harder. I realized another fear – PDA (Public Display of Affection as it was called in my college days) might bring violent reaction. I feared someone would conveniently run them down on a ski slope. I'm very grateful that it never happened. Nor was he ever run off the highway driving back and forth to school with a rainbow sticker (the international gay banner) plastered across his back window. Mothers have fears as well as hopes for their children, and with gay children I think the fears are intensified.

Six years ago we celebrated our son and his partner's commitment ceremony. It was a wedding in all but name and we treated it as such. We had a big hotel ceremony, dinner and a delightful party. Our couples group and some very close friends came to an event that they had never before experienced – two men committing to a life-long covenant of love and support. Our couples group and close friends were living their support; it was a joyous occasion. My husband and I both made toasts celebrating our sons' shared love, their commitment and our guests' public affirmation that there was nothing wrong with two people committing to love and a life-long relationship. After the toasts a thirty-something young man came up to me, put his hands on my shoulders and asked, "Will you be my mother?" Through tears I smiled and hugged him, saying yes, loving him as apparently his own mother had been unable to do. I will always remember this as one of the best, happiest and saddest of moments. I was happy because I thought there might be some healing for him in our family's celebration and my acceptance of him. I was sad because his own mother had rejected her flesh and blood. I was proud because I knew in my own heart that my transition to being the mother of a gay man was complete.

One final thing this celebration showed us; it made us sharply aware of the inequality of the law. In order for our sons' relationship to have what married couples take for granted – like joint ownership of their home and property, power to make medical and end of life decisions – they had to pay large legal fees and sign numerous legal documents. Since this transpired, I am grateful that the state in which they live approved gay marriage. My son and his partner are now legally married.

I wonder if transformation doesn't require some sort of cross. To change or be changed requires struggle – a struggle to let go of a safe way of being. It may not be a fruitful or joyful way of being, but because it's known, it's comfortable and seemingly safe. To change a way of approaching life requires struggle and agony. "Sweating blood," it's sometimes called. Jesus agonized as he accepted the path of transformation; he chose to endure the cross rather than resist or cling to the old way. Should we be surprised that change in us sometimes requires a period of "sweating blood," of feeling lost and of not knowing. Transformation is a kind of cross and perhaps the more it matters, the more it hurts. I know in many different ways, it's worth the joy and the new life on the other side. Once we are transformed, the system in which we live has to shift or change. What has also become evident to me is that a change in me not only affects others, it will either add to or subtract from the good in the world. Perhaps one way to evaluate our changes is whether they do in fact add to the good. I am convinced mine has.

13. A Grandmother-Granddaughter Conversation

"Maybe this is a transition for me, as I step back and realize that my perspective is only one point of view and does not tell the whole story."

Last year as I was searching for a book to read aloud to a fifth grade class, a librarian friend gave me a list of books, and at the top of the list was a book called Wonder by R.J. Palacio. When I tried to order the book from Amazon, I got a message saying that I had purchased the book a year earlier. I mentioned this to my fifth grade granddaughter, Elisabeth.

"Yes, Grandmom. You gave me the book last winter. It's the best book I've ever read. I'm reading it for the third time, but I'm glad to lend it to you when I finish it."

After a couple of days she brought it over, and I began to read. The story is about August Pullman, a boy born with a facial difference causing him to be home-schooled through fourth grade. For his fifth grade year he began attending Beecher Prep, a private school in New York City, and the story centers on Auggie's first year in middle school. The author features perspectives from children who became his friends as well as the ones who ganged up against him.

After a day or so, Elisabeth asked, "What perspective are you on?" It seemed a curious question because I was still in Part I of the book. Palacio develops her story by telling it originally from the perspectives of six characters, and later adding a seventh.

As I read, I realized my understanding of Auggie was much broader because of the perspectives of the other young people, and I wondered how insights into different perspectives lead to transitions in our feelings towards people. Curious about what Elisabeth observed, I decided to ask her how she saw the characters and, in particular, were there any of the characters that she would like to have as friends. (*Elizabeth's responses are in italics.*)

The book begins with August describing himself and explaining what his life had been like from birth to fifth grade.

I would like to be Auggie's friend because he seems to act like all of my real friends. I see Auggie as any other kid that would go to my school; he just has a unique face. He seems very kind. Via, his sister, tells her perspective by describing what it is like to be the older sister of a severely disfigured brother, whom she both loves and resents.

Via could be an okay friend; she's just a little on the dramatic side. On page 88, Via describes Auggie's face. It gave me a better understanding of what he looked like.

Then five of Auggie's friends share their perspectives. First, Summer describes how she became his friend. On the first day of school without adult encouragement, she set her lunch tray on the table where Auggie was sitting alone. She sat down and began chatting.

I think Summer would be a GREAT friend because she's very loyal and treats people the way she wants to be treated.

The next perspective comes from Jack. Jack met Auggie in the summer when the director of Beecher Prep, Mr. Tushman, asked three students to come to school and show Auggie around. Jack and Auggie ended up sitting beside each other in several classes, and Jack began to depend on Auggie's help with his schoolwork. This was truly helpful for Jack, because school was difficult for him.

I learned from Jack how smart Auggie was. Jack could be an okay friend; he was just kind of reluctant to hang out with Auggie, unlike Summer.

The last two perspectives are from Via's boyfriend, Justin, and her BFF, (until high school), Miranda. They are both very accepting of Auggie; in fact, Miranda adores him.

Justin didn't really talk very much about Auggie; he pretty much just talked about Via. Justin would be a pretty good friend because he's a musician. Miranda would be a really awesome friend because she's really fun and spunky. Miranda hangs out with August a lot and seems to have fun with him. I noticed that Auggie seemed not to be as shy as he was at the beginning of the book. When he goes on his class trip, he has a campfire, and when I went on mine, there was a REALLY FUN campfire there. When Auggie and his mom were packing, it reminded me of my fifth grade trip. Auggie's mom was being very overprotective, just like mine.

My perspective changed DRASTICALLY about Miles, Henry and Amos. (These three boys in the class had been hateful to Auggie all year. Julian, the leader of the gang trying to get rid of Auggie, was not on the class trip.)

"How about Julian? What do you think about him now that we've been able to 'hear' his side of the story?"

I honestly think that Julian was sort of jumping on the bandwagon. He just did everything his mom did, which was to dislike Auggie.

"Are you glad Ms. Palacio added this section?"

I am SOOOOOOOOO happy she added this perspective. It adds a whole new opinion on Julian for me.

I recently noticed thoughts about the book come up when I found myself being somewhat irritated by a lack of gratitude from a friend of mine. I thought of my conversations with Elisabeth, so I sought to listen from her perspective. I remembered Wonder and the perspectives it teaches. Maybe this is a transition for me, as I step back and realize that my perspective is only one point of view and does not tell the whole story.

"Elisabeth, do you see yourself responding or reacting differently to people as a result of learning the different ways these characters respond or react to Auggie?"

I guess so. I mean there aren't really any special needs people at my school. But, when a new girl transferred to Kittridge, my two other friends and I made sure she felt welcome. The four of us are now good friends.

"One thing we need to talk about is how this story may have changed us even though you don't have special needs students at Kittridge, and neither of us has known someone as disfigured as Auggie. I consider my recent frustration with a friend when I realized that I was not really listening to her perspective of what happened. The story reminded me that she saw it very differently from me. This made me rethink my earlier take on what happened. Though this is something I noticed in what happened to me, I wonder if this is something which holds true for you."

You know, Grandmom, I have always known not to judge a book by its cover, so that honestly did not change me much. What really changed my thoughts after reading Wonder is that you don't really know someone until you discover that they really are just like you.

14. Facing Death and New Life: a Grandmother's Reflection

"Being human brings a mixture of joy and sorrow, yet love binds it all together. Each moment we can choose to pause, breathe deep, and take refuge in presence and love."

With awe, reverence, and indescribable joy, I can now say that I'm a grandmother. The blessing of this transition is intensified for me in knowing that my own dear mother was never graced with holding her grandbaby during the time she walked this good earth. I continue *to live the questions* through this fragile and uncertain journey called life, yet I can hold the paradox of joy meeting sorrow, and the ways in which losing both my parents before my twenty-first birthday continues to engage ever deeper wellsprings of connection to what matters most.

The miracle of new birth is just that – a miracle! I still remember how the birth of my three children evoked a deep sense of unconditional love and connection that springs forth in a flash. The moment they were born, I was overtaken by a mixture of amazement, awe, trepidation, and hope. Though they are all adults now, I continue to feel like my heart is somehow walking around outside of me. My husband and I still feel wonder, delight, and heartbreak as we watch them grow. Clearly, motherhood brings unique joys and sorrows, and getting older has a way of softening the edges as life's journey deepens the awareness of all that's grand in parenting.

The unfolding years allowed me to accept the truth of life's uncertainty, along with the infinite possibilities that come through the goodness and mercy that follow us. As I live into this new and vital transition of grandparenting, I'm reminded that each day brings new invitations to *let go and let God*. The journey from daughter to mother to grandmother is touching, wondrous, and bittersweet, and it invites me to pause and reflect on *my story*.

Facing Death without Warning

One particular morning in my thirteenth year, I was busy doing all the things most young girls do while getting ready for school. On what seemed to be an ordinary day, I had no idea how my life would change in an instant. While primping and pondering what to wear that day, I noticed a strange noise coming from the room at the end of the hall where my mother and father slept. I was confused by the sound because I knew my mom was in the kitchen cooking breakfast, and I thought my dad had already left for work. This odd, gurgling noise was growing in intensity until it drew me down the hall and into their room. When I entered the room, I saw my father lying on the bed gasping for breath. I went to him and sought to give him mouth-to-mouth resuscitation (no CPR classes in those days). I didn't know what to do, yet I was able to follow my instincts. I worked diligently to get air into his lungs, struggling to help him overcome his compulsive gasping for air. All of this was to no avail, and I found myself holding my father when he drew his last breath. In a matter of minutes, I went from being an ordinary thirteen-year-old to living through the most traumatic transition in my life. After my father died in my arms, the rest of the morning was mostly a blur, though I do remember my mother sobbing as she called for an ambulance. Soon our neighborhood was filled with activity; the ambulance came and the medics dashed into the house, and I felt both frightened and helpless. Though I had done all that I could, it was not enough.

In the aftermath of this trauma, I remember distinctly my mother's strength even in the midst of her shock, fear, and sadness. For a short time she was crying out of control, yet it wasn't long before she began to calm down and console me and my brother. Her urge to protect us offers a stunning example of the courage and love so instinctively alive in mothering. We connected with hugs and tears and words of affirmation and hope. This togetherness not only occurred on the day of my father's passing, but during the weeks that followed.

After this harrowing experience our family came together to begin the long process of acceptance and healing. As we were experiencing our grief, friends and neighbors poured into our house sharing their feelings and support. In the midst of the chaos and grief, the gracious people around us offered love and caring; even though I was experiencing a great sense of loss, their love gave me a strange and beautiful feeling of being held and sustained. Those feelings of being held, loved and supported in the midst of tears and sadness stayed with me for days and weeks following my father's passing. Our family lost him to a heart attack at forty-nine years of age, and this loss imprinted on my heart a deep knowing that life is fragile and precious. Further, my mother's response left an even deeper imprint, as she reassured our family that while we don't know what the next moment will bring, we do know that love will always surround us. We must simply open our eyes and our hearts.

How ironic that the death of my father opened my eyes to see clearly the faith and resilience of my mother. Through her deep grief and sadness she assured me that with God's help, everything would be okay. Her devoted strength and deep joy sustained me throughout my high school years and to the day of her death, which also came too soon.

Her bright spirit is alive in me still, and it inspired me as I reared my own children. As I consider the ominous responsibility of raising two teenagers alone, I now wonder if my mother did not cry herself to sleep many a night while I slept securely. A fragmented, superficial person could not have endured what she suffered. My mother's love grew deeper and more vibrant as she embraced her friends and family, and served her church joyfully. Those years following my father's death were happy years in spite of our loss. Surrounded by loving family and friends, I moved with seeming ease from high school to college.

Facing Death Again, and Too Soon

While attending college I fell deeply in love with my high school sweetheart (sappy, but true!), and my college journey was filled with adventures in learning and fun. Life was rocking along until the summer before I completed my student teaching and graduated. Though not as sudden as my father's death, I had to face the fact that my mother's life would also end too soon.

I remember sitting beside her bed at Piedmont Hospital, knowing that she was seriously ill but not accepting that she might die. For some reason she was never able to tell me directly how ill she really was. She said that she had anemia, but I knew it was much more serious than that. I instinctively accepted her limited willingness to share the truth of her acute leukemia, and I didn't allow that to rob us of sacred bedside moments of connection. This was her journey and her transition from the mystery of this life. By the grace of God, I knew my part during her transition through death was to simply be a loving presence.

Naturally, as I watched her energy dissipate, I felt a growing sadness; but even in her dying, her resilient spirit and love shined through. Though her body was losing its battle with leukemia, she exuded a sense of strength until she breathed her last breath. When I lost her, I was at once deeply saddened, yet filled with a sense of being all wrapped up in God's love. Though she is not with me in body today, her loving spirit is with me still. The memory of her radiant smile sustained me through her death, and it continues to strengthen my faith and sustain me in my unfolding journey. Strangely enough, losing my mom opened me to feel evermore rooted and grounded in God's love and grace. In the midst of grief, I was able to touch that peace that passes understanding and trust that no matter what happens, I could walk through it. By keeping my heart open rather than hardening it in the tough moments, I can lean into the love that surrounds me. The loss of both of my parents before I finished college has made me aware of the fragility and beauty of life. To this day, I consciously seek to appreciate every moment that I breathe life on this earth, and I cannot imagine that I would have cultivated this awareness and gratitude without experiencing the loss of my father and mother. Further, the example of my mother's transition through grief has left me with a deep conviction that no matter what happens in this strange medley of life, there is always a power present to hold us. If we keep our hearts open, there is always someone we can count on to ground us in love. We need each other, and life is richer when we are surrounded by those who will both weep with us and rejoice with us.

Rejoicing in New Life as I Become a Grandmother

I rejoice in being a grandparent, and I cannot imagine a more stunning transition. The sacred moment of experiencing new life as I held my grandson in the delivery room will forever be imprinted on my heart. It was as though my emotions were pure and unfiltered, and the tears flowed almost like a firehose. I've heard it said that those sudden flashes of tears invite a glimpse of eternity, and this "flash flood" of tears offered me vivid evidence of an ever-flowing stream of God's grace and love. My salty tears were a mixture of wonder, humility, awe, reverence, joy, and a peace that passes understanding as I sensed my own mother and father rejoicing with me. Even now, I can taste those salty tears that catch the flow of all tears and stir up sighs of gratitude along with a love that flows too deep for words. Savoring moments like this can illuminate our very lives, as they reveal the stunning beauty and goodness of being human. Further, they invite us to open up to deeper truths woven into the mysteries, marvels, and even the messes of life.

My life's story reminds me to never take for granted the promise of new life. I continue to live into knowing that all of life is transition, and the circumstances of life can change in a flash. Being human brings a mixture of joy and sorrow, yet love binds it all together. Each moment we can choose to pause, breathe deep, and take refuge in presence and love. No matter how deep the pain, if we wait long enough, God will bring a blessing. I can see the unmistakable blessings of life as I tenderly hold my precious grandson and look into his bright eyes. I trust in the hope that shines as I reflect on the moment I witnessed my son become a father– WOW!! Grandbabies – all you need to do is hold one, or witness your baby son or daughter hold one, to know how heaven feels!!

15. Facing Retirement

"I do feel fulfilled to have contributed to the common good, and I hope in some small way it has made a difference in the world."

My story feels pretty common to me, not a lot of flash and color, nothing to make a person jealous of my setting or work or goals. Whether or not my story stirs any excitement in others, it is, nevertheless, my story, the only story that I have to offer. For that reason I want to share it with others who may feel much like I do.

The story I want to share focuses on my retirement, which I am considering and which is already partly underway. To tell my story I am beginning with my present setting, where I am and what I am doing on a daily basis. But I will then describe my background and training and my first job. My story weaves its way from New Jersey to Maryland and finally to Atlanta, Georgia, where I now live and have spent the last forty years. My vocation for over forty years has been in the field of nursing. It has taken me unexpectedly to different employers and to additional training. From this stage I am considering retirement.

Present Engagement

I am presently working in the School of Nursing at Emory University where I supervise the clinical training of nurses and nurse practitioners. The most rewarding aspect of my work has been the relationship that I develop with students. In the past, most undergraduate nursing students would choose nursing as their first undergraduate degree. But recently, about half of the students beginning their undergraduate nursing already have a bachelor's degree in a different major, so we have been getting different kinds of persons in the program. Many have had jobs in other fields, and then decided they wanted to be a nurse or nurse practitioner. When these persons come to us for training, they are highly motivated and very eager to succeed, so they study hard, work hard, and become committed professionals.

At first there was a great deal of resistance to bringing this type of student into our program. Those who were creating and supervising the nursing curriculum had the opinion that students needed practical experience prior to entering the program. These students usually came to us in their middle twenties with a plan of what they want to do and how they want to become a nurse practitioner. They are interested in advanced training so that they can provide either primary care or more care, for example, nurse midwifery and critical care. These have made some of our very best nurses. One of my past responsibilities was to find doctors and nurse practitioners who are willing to have students in clinical settings.

When these new students first enter the program, it is my task to assign them to a place where they can gain practical, hands-on experience. I see them during their first semester heart assessment class and experience the delight they feel when they are able to take blood pressure or draw a blood sample from a client. After getting them started in a clinic and seeing them begin to develop, I don't see them again until they have completed the first year of work and are beginning the graduate nursing program. I'm always amazed at how they have changed, how much enthusiasm they express about nursing and how seriously they are engaged in their preparation. Seeing these changes occur has been a very rewarding experience for me. One of the classes that I coordinated was Advanced Health Assessment, and teaching gave me a closer relationship with the students. Afterward, I was assigned to follow them through their clinical experience. Passing through all the stages of admission, preparation, instruction and seeing the development of these new students caused me to celebrate having a share in their becoming nurse practitioners.

For example, I recall having one student who was about forty years of age. She had recently gone through a divorce and had remarried a man with a couple of children; she had a family of five children with the marriage. She had her hands full just taking care of this family and developing a relationship with her new husband. Yet, she applied herself to her course of study diligently and I was very, very proud of her and felt personally rewarded. Every day along with taking her courses she had to coordinate those kids, taking them where they needed to go, get her husband off to work and take care of her academic responsibilities. She was exceptionally bright and did an excellent job in all these responsibilities.

After having a successful career and enjoying the benefits of my work through these years, how could I ever want to retire? To answer that question, all I have to do is recall how tired I have felt some mornings when I wake up.

My Background

My life began in a small town in New Jersey where my father worked as both a bank teller and a salesman, and my mother was a receptionist in a real estate office. I grew up in a very innocent, protected environment, and I was rather naïve about the rest of the world. My town was so small that the high school which I attended was a town or two away. Every day I rode the school bus from my home to the school, about five miles to the east.

Choosing a Vocation after Graduation

In that era the most common vocations open for women were teaching, nursing, or becoming a secretary. I had never taken a typing class and my family had little money, so I pretty much backed into my nursing career.

After graduating from high school, a cousin sent me information about a nursing diploma offered at Johns Hopkins Hospital. As I look back at my situation, going down to investigate Johns Hopkins University and making a decision about the direction of my work life has some strange twists to it. I had a very good friend whose uncle lived in Baltimore, and she said that we could stay in his house if we wished to explore the Johns Hopkins diploma. At the time I had never heard of Johns Hopkins, and I'm amazed at the way I discovered it. Because of the generosity of my friend's uncle, she and I rode the train from New Jersey down to Maryland, where we had a free room and a clean bed. We arrived, got settled and decided to go over to the university to see what it was like. It is somewhat humorous to me today when I remember how impressed I was at those students we met walking around in white jackets; some had stethoscopes hanging around their necks. Shortly after seeing these uniformed students, we walked past a swimming pool where other students were sunning and swimming. The thought of having our own swimming pool in which we could actually go swimming was an attraction to both of us. A few days later we decided to apply for the diploma in nursing.

Today I'm shocked at the superficial judgment that got me into my lifelong work. Yet, with all the superficiality with which I approached this program, I can confirm today that this really was the right place for me. This is how a seventeen-year-old girl makes a rather large decision about her vocation. Johns Hopkins seemed so big and challenging that I wanted to undertake it.

Later as I thought about this decision, I recalled how impressed I was with all those people wearing little white coats everywhere they went; it seemed to me a good thing to be identified with people like them. During all this time I was so radically uninformed about Johns Hopkins, I did not realize what a reputation this university had in the field of medicine. Instead of reveling in the superiority of this university, I was amazed at lesser things like white jackets and a swimming pool. In three years I did receive the diploma and began my career.

My First Job

After graduating from Johns Hopkins Hospital, I worked at Hopkins for two years. I had some acquaintances in Atlanta and after those two years, I decided to get out of the cold and move into a warmer climate. One of my best friends at Hopkins was from Atlanta, so I decided to go there. This friend had a job at Emory, and she told me that they were hiring nurses in the Coronary Care Unit. After I had been at Emory for a few years, I began to look around for an opportunity to switch to public health nursing. I applied to several clinics in the county and soon got a job. There was one hitch. In order to get the job that I really wanted, I had to get a bachelor's degree because they would not accept the diploma from Hopkins.

I began studying part-time at Georgia State University and in three years had accumulated enough credits to get my bachelor's degree in nursing. When I first entered Georgia State University, I had a somewhat unpleasant experience. The professors forced us to wear blue student nurse uniforms. Most of us were resentful to be treated like a novice when we had already been working as Registered Nurses. I worked all day on the floor of the hospital taking care of patients, and then I had to take off my RN uniform and put on one of those silly student uniforms. After three years with the degree in hand, I was able to get employment with the DeKalb County Health Department.

Working in Public Health

I worked four years as a public health nurse in DeKalb County. I loved public health nursing. I daily reported to the main center and from there served multiple sites throughout the county. Our primary tasks were well-child checks and women's health. In addition to the patient work in the clinic, we made home visits. We especially visited homes where there were new babies. We helped the new mom with questions that she might be asking, and we examined the newborn baby. We did a vast amount of teaching of pregnant women that included providing information, supervision and oversight throughout the pregnancy and delivery. Most of our babies were delivered at Grady Hospital. There were many, many pregnant women who came from the poorer strata of society who desperately needed our care. In addition to this individual care, we had classes on how to care for newborns, how to feed properly and the need for rest to keep up the mothers' strength. Actually, the care that we gave these women was better than I ever got at a private doctor's office.

Further Training Still

After four years working for DeKalb County, I decided that I wanted to increase my skills so I could provide more in-depth care for my patients. I applied to Vanderbilt University in Nashville, Tennessee for admission to receive a master's degree as a Family Nurse Practitioner. Fortunately I got a scholarship that paid my tuition, purchased my books and provided me a small stipend to cover my living expenses. The only requirement was that after graduation I give two years of service to an under-served population. Vanderbilt was only four hours from Atlanta, so I traveled back and forth to keep up my relationships. If I got a little homesick while I was at Vanderbilt, I could refresh myself with a short visit to Atlanta. When I completed my training at Vanderbilt, there were numerous clinics where I could pay back the service that I owed the government. One option was to work on an Indian reservation, but I was a bit hesitant, not wanting to live so far from my Atlanta friends.

After having been away from Atlanta for a couple of years, I began to realize that I had deep roots in the city. So as I was researching possibilities for my two years of service, I discovered that the State of Georgia offered opportunities for my service stint. I had an interview with the public health department to see if I could get employment to serve as my two-year commitment. I did get a qualifying job with the state and wound up in Athens, Georgia working in under-served county health departments. After completing my two years of service, I decided to move back to Atlanta and find a job.

Unexpected Doors Open
A new interest in Atlanta inspired me to burn up the highway between Atlanta and Athens to spend time with my husband-to-be. In order to get back to Atlanta, I worked with several public health agencies on a per diem basis to get enough money to live on. I had not been in Atlanta too long before I found myself working again for DeKalb County in public health. In 1983 I got married and had my first child in 1985. I did not want to go back to work full-time while my daughter was young. Fortunately, through my job with the state I had accumulated a great deal of leave time, three months in fact. With these accumulated days, without working I received a salary for three months while I was caring for my newborn.

In the first few months of my daughter's life, a friend of mine came to visit and get acquainted with her and offer her support. By this time I was already thinking about part-time employment. In the course of our conversation, she indicated that Emory was now hiring people with my qualifications in pediatrics and women's health. My friend suggested that I apply for this position. I did apply and got the job, thinking at the time that it would only be temporary. Twenty-six years later I am still there, though the demands of the job included teaching and I had never thought of myself as an academic. Even though I was employed by Emory, I continued working at the county health department. This taught me a big lesson about doors opening when a person is receptive. Consequently, I've always encouraged my students to keep an open mind about where they are going, because you never know what doors will open and where you will be needed

.

Reflection on Twenty-Six Years

During my twenty-six years at Emory, I had a variety of responsibilities. I began supervising nurse practitioners, coordinating classes and finding clinical sites at which nurses could be trained on a one-to-one basis. I have to say that finding good sites is one of the toughest jobs in the world. I coordinated the Family Nurse Practitioner program on an interim basis for several years. I could not apply for this job on a permanent basis because I did not have a Ph.D. One of my colleagues did go back to school to get her doctorate and then assumed the job. I wanted to stay full-time, so I began doing classes with undergraduates as well as graduates. I wanted to remain a full-time employee at Emory because I liked the work, and there were generous educational rewards. I thought about getting a Ph.D., but truthfully, I did not want to go back to school again, especially at an older age. I don't particularly care for research, nor do I feel an interest in scholarly writing, and to get a Ph.D. would have required both. Always in my evaluations I got low marks on academic endeavors like research, writing and publishing. So, I decided to stay in the field that allowed me to do the things I love to do most. I had enough experience, knowledge and skills to do a variety of clinically related teaching, but I chose to remain with what brought me the greatest fulfillment, so I bypassed the Ph.D. Quite honestly, at that time in my life being involved in my daughter's education and activities was my priority.

On the Personal Side

As our family increased, I began to experience a spiritual awakening. After graduating from nursing school there were quite a few years that I didn't go to church at all. When my first daughter came along, I wanted her to be reared in the church, with the hope that she would acquire the values that the church teaches. In addition to instruction and modeling in our home, in the church we would have dozens of other people helping us rear our children too.

After moving to a new neighborhood, we enrolled our two and a half-year-old daughter in a preschool program at a nearby church. We wanted her to be involved in Sunday school and the choirs, but I could not expect her to benefit from these activities without being a role model and attending the church myself. I have most appreciated that our church is like an adopted family. I feel that I belong, that I have responsibilities and that I have a number of friends who love and support me no matter what happens in my life. Most of our good friends are members of our church. So the church is not only a place of spiritual instruction, teaching and worship, but it is also a source of finding our best and dearest friends. I really feel sorry for the people who do not have this kind of support system.

God's Unrecognized Presence

As I look back over my life, I have a strange sense that there has been a Providence operative in the decisions, encounters and occurrences that at the time I was totally unaware of. I suppose it is something like experiencing the invisible hand of God shaping my life, when I was not thinking of God at all. The cousin who sent me information about Johns Hopkins, my friend who had an uncle in Baltimore and was also willing to take the trip with me, the silly attraction of the white coats and the swimming pool, the impossibility to advance in my vocation without an accredited degree and the doors that the degree opened to me, a desire to be of more value and more service, which took me for a master's degree at Vanderbilt University, getting a job at Emory affecting the lives of our students, which gave me such inward satisfaction, the shift from public health to an academic institution, which provided education for my children. All of these seemingly natural events, which I don't believe were accidental, have shaped my life.

And now I have a sense that it's time for me to retire. Is this also a manifestation of the divine presence? Because of my employment at Emory, both of my daughters got a courtesy scholarship, meaning that their basic degree cost us nothing. How many hundreds of thousands of dollars would it have taken to buy this quality education! All of these occurrences suggest to me that there is and has been a divine presence in the unfolding of my life.

I am still a work in progress. I'm trying to listen more. My youngest daughter has decided she wants to be a nurse. She just finished her third semester taking pre-requisite science classes, and she still has chemistry classes, which she is not looking forward to. There are certainly challenges in the nursing profession these days, but I am honored and very proud this daughter has chosen the same profession that I have followed. She is a very gifted person: she is compassionate; she loves people; she is very self-giving. When she decided to go back to school, her employer promised a challenging reward for every A that she made in her studies. She's trying to break the bank!

Living the Questions of Retirement

Nursing has gone through so many changes the last few years. These changes, plus the additional stress they incur, have caused me to think seriously about retirement. I know that I cannot completely retire at this time because of the financial implications, but, at least, I have begun to consider it. At the university there is a much stronger emphasis on the scholastic aspects within the nursing faculty and less interest in practical skills. Consequently, I began to lose some of my passion for continuing to work. Not only was there a stronger emphasis on the academics, but all of us were encouraged to do research, to write and to publish articles in nursing journals. There seemed to be more emphasis on the cognitive development of nurses than the practical nursing experiences. While I am not critical of this shift in emphasis, it has focused attention on things I am least interested in.

My concern throughout the years of my career has been serving people. Since it seemed to me that these recent changes were moving nursing in a different direction, I began to think more often about retirement. What has kept me from retiring has been my need for a monthly income. I needed to work, but the work that I was being asked to do did not draw on my strongest gifts and left me feeling underused. Added to this was the frustration with leadership. Some of the people to whom I've reported did not plan ahead, nor organize well. They made too many decisions without sufficient planning. I do not flourish in that kind of environment. This way of leadership frustrates me and puts me under a great deal of stress.

I recently decided to cut back my time to fifty percent for the entire academic year. I'm really happy with this decision; it does not totally cut me off from the work that I had been doing for years, but by cutting back I have retired halfway. Retiring in stages is something like diving into the deep end of the pool and swimming until you can touch the bottom. From that point, it is step-by-step to the shallow end, and the final step is out of the pool completely. At Emory, in order to have insurance coverage it is necessary for me to be engaged at least fifty percent of the time, and having medical benefits is a very important aspect for me. Naturally, I miss the fifty percent of income that I'm not receiving, but we will find ways to make it in retirement. My target is to be fully retired by the end of next summer, nine months away. I have been careful not to discuss this with any of my colleagues or supervisors because I want to keep my options open and not burn bridges I may need to cross again.

Life Reflection

As I review the past forty-five years of my life, I believe that I have made a difference through my vocation. As I reflect on my career, I have shown compassion and a spirit of helpfulness to hundreds of people; I have taught scores of women about the responsibility of motherhood and childcare; I have participated in educating hundreds of young people who have wanted to become nurses; and I have contributed to helping build a positive environment in the workplace. When I think about the contribution I have made to the common good, I don't want to overlook the fact that I have been part of a church where I have worked in mission projects, helped the needy, and I have dedicated my efforts to help my children have meaningful, productive lives. Through my parenthood, my work and my volunteer service I have hopefully made life better for others and for myself. I do feel fulfilled to have contributed to the common good, and I hope in some small way it has made a difference in the world.

As I look toward the future, I hope to have time to have fun with friends, to do things with them that I cannot do while I'm working. But I also look forward to volunteering my time to things that deeply interest me, like holding classes for refugee mothers-to-be and teaching them how to be good mothers. This would be fulfilling and I think it would meet a genuine need. I also hope to get involved with other mission projects in our community – perhaps a food bank and mother's morning out program.

Some might think that having had all my experience in nursing that I would want to volunteer as a nurse, but that is not true for me. When I nurse people, I have a deep sense of responsibility for their health and well-being, and that is a stress I want to avoid in retirement.

If I could do something in education, like support or advise students, I would be happy to do it. But maybe selfishly, I do not want the responsibility of someone's health.

In the last few years, I have volunteered my service at a clinic in downtown Atlanta , a women's shelter where there is a lack of organization and funding. This experience brought a great deal of frustration to me. Unfortunately, there is a lack of follow-through. This clinic also struggles to meet the needs of clients, which are overwhelming; the needs are much greater than the organization could possibly respond to.

I hope the future provides me an opportunity to work with refugees. I have a deep interest in the refugees in Clarkston, Georgia. Every Thursday evening I join with a dozen other people to pack bags of food to be distributed to children who would not otherwise have a meal over the weekend. My heart is deeply moved by this situation, and my sense of compassion is such that I feel I must be involved in this good work.

As I evaluate my life, my greatest struggles have been with stress. My struggle has been to keep from worrying and to trust that all things will work together for good in my life. I definitely could use more of a *"let go and let God"* attitude. Over and over I have found myself struggling with conflicting attitudes toward people and situations.

Another struggle for me has been follow-through. Often I say that I'm going to do this or that, then fail to follow through. I don't appreciate this behavior in myself or in other people. I hope that my follow-through in this next chapter of my life will be all about making a difference through service, so while I'll "retire" one area of service, I'll be open to new possibilities beyond nursing and Emory.

16. Fired or Retired?

"The God who created the mountains and held the earth together in an earthquake and made the trees grow and the flowers bloom could surely take care of me and my family."

I remember the day like it was yesterday. It was the fifth day of May in 2007. That day is etched in my mind like a name and date chiseled on a tombstone. I got a letter from my employer, Hewlett-Packard, telling me that I could retire early; they offered me a good exit with a thick cushion that would see me through the first year. When I read this notice, a chill went through my whole being. I experienced a mixture of delight and anxiety along with hopefulness and despair. The days and weeks that followed were filled with turmoil as I wrestled with the decision whether to take the generous offer or to refuse it.

As the days passed, the pressure mounted. Regularly I got emails requesting me to make the decision and inform my superiors of my decision. Every week I had to go online and check the box that said "Yes, I am retiring" or "No, I am staying." I had to ask myself if I'm not working for Hewlett-Packard, what am I going to do with myself? Will I have the security that I need for myself and my family if I leave this job?

When I shared this information with my wife, her first questions were, "How will we live? How will we educate our children? How secure are we for the future if you leave Hewlett-Packard?" For several weeks she and I mulled over the opportunity; we shared both the anxiety and the excitement of being free to do some of the things that we had always dreamed about doing.

My wife and I were on our way to the mountains of North Georgia to visit with friends for the weekend when I made the final decision. The picture is stamped in my mind, as prior to the trip we had said "No" one day and "Yes" the next. As we were driving through the mountains, we passed by a Starbucks where I stopped, ran in and called my boss and said the final "Yes." Yes, I am choosing to retire. I still did not feel confident in the decision, but I finally said, "Why not?" After making that decision, I recall arriving at the cabin, looking out at the beauty of the mountains and trying to convince myself that life would be good and that my family and I would be safe. The God who created the mountains and held the earth together in an earthquake and made the trees grow and the flowers bloom could surely take care of me and my family.

My Path to Hewlett-Packard

After I knew that I was leaving Hewlett-Packard, I began to review my life decision in college and how that prepared me for the work that I had done for the past forty-five years. I had worked with Hewlett-Packard for seventeen years. Prior to that I had been part of two other similar companies – Digital Equipment Corporation and Compaq. Eventually these two companies merged with Hewlett-Packard. I grew with the mergers and wound up spending over forty-five years working in this field.

As I looked more deeply into the influences that finally brought me to the Information Technology field, I recalled beginning college studying electrical engineering. After a couple of years in that program I began to see that I did not match up with this field of endeavor. Perhaps calculus in my second year solidified my decision. That subject simply did not make sense to me – my gifts and interest made me aware that I did not want to sit behind a desk working on formulas that I did not understand. Although I was adapting to the world of engineering, I was not at all fulfilled, and I was not excited by my studies.

While I was struggling with preparing for a desk job and calculus, I discovered that I could transfer into a degree program in Business Management. By making this move I began to feel more comfortable. I quickly learned that Business Management was a lot more fun for me, and this new field gave me images of possibilities that I had never seen before. Business Management was not primarily about thinking but rather a combination of research and reflection, plus my own imagination and creativity. This approach to business had a very different appeal to me, plus it seemed to match the skills, talents and gifts that I had. Since Business Management was not so theoretical, so exact, so cut and dried, it just opened a whole new set of doors for me.

Business Management showed me that I am really a complex person, a divided person with two complementary parts. I have a logical, very well organized side, and I also have the opposite, which is creative, artistic and imaginative. I discovered a strength that I was not always aware of, but when I began to work at effective management of people and processes, I found a new and deeper delight. The demands of this work brought heretofore hidden gifts to the forefront, gifts that helped make me a success.

I spent most of my years in a technical business, basically in a marketing position. I sat on one side or the other of the negotiation table either seeking to sell a client or purchase from a provider. I always tried to get the negotiations to a place that made everyone happy with the decision.

A Fresh Perspective on Memories of Hewlett-Packard

Making the decision to retire early and to seek a less demanding form of employment and to develop my personal interests gave me an opportunity to review the things that I liked most about being under the Hewlett-Packard umbrella. As I review my years working in the IT world, I think the greatest gift that I brought to my work was a sensitivity to people. I truly believe that something inside of me cared about the thoughts, feelings, desires, and ambitions of the people I worked with. I didn't at first recognize this gift, but after years of experience I see this aspect of myself more clearly. This view of and feelings for others came to the forefront for me even in marketing and sales. I attended numerous seminars, conferences and short courses on personality types and how to relate differently to each type, but generally I found these principles embedded in me. I seemed to have been born with them; what was needed was situations to bring them out. At the seminars I learned names for the practices that I had already adopted. I am not discounting the experiences of these human relation seminars because they did introduce me to the various people types, ways of relating honestly and clearly with them, and how to keep relationships open. Gaining clarity and good definitions was extremely helpful.

How I related to my clients was very simple; it was a matter of building trust. This basic principle held true whether I was seeking to serve a client or buy from a provider. Good, positive relationships meant everything to me. My goal was always to create a win–win situation where we trusted each other and sought to find middle ground when it came to price and quality. Every time I came to a common understanding with both a client and a provider, I felt fulfilled inside. This state of relationships was at the core of my work and what mattered to me.

Unexpected Sources of Satisfaction

As I reappraise my years at Hewlett-Packard, one of the most rewarding experiences of my life had nothing to do with my business. As a representative of my company, I was flying all over the world. When I traveled, I had the privilege of sitting in first class or business class on the long international trips. On almost every trip I found myself sitting by a man who, like me, was traveling the world for his company. After getting acquainted and having a few drinks, my seatmate would begin generally to tell me all the things he struggled with. I listened carefully and responded appropriately; in some instances, friendships developed that lasted longer than the plane ride. And this showed me that I had a gift for listening and understanding the deeper feelings and needs of another person. You can only help people after listening to and understanding them. For people to reveal themselves to you, they must feel safe in your presence because they are dealing with vulnerable issues in their lives. The people with whom I was flying were all very busy people who had needs in their lives that did not go away when they left home; there was no place to run, no place to fly to get away.

I sought to be a listener and offer whatever I could to get through their problem. Sitting with people and sharing my life with them as they shared theirs with me gave me such deep satisfaction, and I was not even paid to perform this service.

After landing in a new place and engaging a person from another culture, I was a listener and a learner also. I listened and sought to relate openly and honestly with whatever client I was speaking with wherever I was in the world. One of the first things that I attempted when I found myself in a different culture was to learn a few words of a different language. I listened and honored people who were different from me, and this made a difference in all that I was doing. I always wanted to be close to the people I was working with. I wanted them to perceive me as a friend and helper, rather than a threat or a manipulator. I generally asked them to help me express my appreciation or my need for direction. I wanted to help my client smile, laugh and generally appreciate our interaction with each other. This attitude and practice always helped me get to know my client better. In those years when I was a global representative for my company, I visited almost every area of the world with the exception of Africa, China and India. I particularly knew all the countries of Europe quite well.

I have also come to appreciate from my time at Hewlett-Packard the challenges my bosses gave me. I'm the kind of person who loves to be challenged with new things, new concepts and new ideas. In the field of Information Technology there are so many facets that stir the curiosity within me. My company thrived on my interest in learning; I received strong support; I could name what I wanted to learn, and funds were usually available for me to explore my interest. Every time I learned some new application, I asked myself how I could put it to use to serve my client and my company better. Usually when I made some new discovery, I stayed fascinated with it for a while, but then I needed something new to keep me challenged and growing.

Regrets about Retirement

My greatest regret about retiring was that I felt like I was fired. In the end my feeling of loss was just as great as it would have been had I been fired outright. I remember that feeling of rejection that came upon me when I was invited to retire. I accept responsibility for making the decision to leave, but because I was not confident, I was very anxious. For the longest time I felt like I had been thrown out of a company that I helped to build. Even though I had been very successful in my life, though I had never lost a job and never lacked work to do, being invited to leave was a blow to my ego. For the life of me, I cannot explain this deep feeling of rejection though the decision proved the best thing for me.

Six months later Hewlett-Packard had another downsizing, and I'm certain that I would have been included in that round of lay-offs had I not taken advantage of the generous offer I was given. I left Hewlett in 2007 just when the economic downturn took place. We went through one of the greatest depressions since the 1920s. In that environment I began looking for a job to bolster my family's security.

Securing Another Job

After deciding to retire from Hewlett-Packard, I worked hard for six months with an outplacement organization. I spent hours analyzing my strengths and preferences deciding what I wanted to do. While I was looking for a new company to work with, I got an opportunity to connect with a software company. The woman in charge of this company had been a former employee of Hewlett-Packard. Her new company needed to revise its supplier-management relationship. It only took a brief look to recognize that this fledgling company was really struggling with this issue. Though it took me six months to find this job, I really liked and respected the woman who headed it. She was very good at her job. I went to work for half the money I had been making, but it was a job and I was happy to stop looking for employment. I wound up staying with this company for three years. After the woman who hired me left, relationships began to go downhill. My gifts in forming good relations with suppliers seemed to be taken for granted, and this led to deteriorating relationships. My new boss was a micro-manager; she wanted a report of all my activities, where I went and what I did. She sought to learn how to make deals that saved the company money. She and others questioned me intensely about my approach and how I negotiated the deals. I soon recognized that I was being used to train them to take my job. As soon as they knew what I knew, I became unnecessary or, as they say in England, redundant. What they could not duplicate were the relationships that I had built in the industry over forty-five years. I knew the costs and the profit margins, and I always played fair with the supplier

The person who hired me stayed for about a year and then left. After she left, things turned sour. My interest also declined. From my vantage point, the leadership of the company lacked integrity and failed to be open in all their dealings. On one occasion I had the distinct feeling that one of the principals was taking kickbacks from some of our clients. This behavior was certainly unacceptable, and I did not want to be associated with it. I probably would have quit much earlier if it had not been for that one person whom I really admired who offered strong, positive leadership to the organization. She was funny. She was happy. She knew how to get the job done. She knew how to take an older employee like myself and let him do his work. When she left, my new boss wanted to know everything I did and when I did it. I felt I was being treated like a child.

The new head of the company accused me of giving confidential information to a supplier. I have no recollection of this ever happening; it is an act that I would not tolerate in myself. Nevertheless, he put me on probation. I am disappointed that my last job was not that fulfilling at all. After just a few months under this new management, I was ready to leave the company; then on December 7, 2010 my supervisor came to my desk and asked me to leave the premises. I was given permission to return and claim my records and personal items the next day. Then I was told that as of that moment I was fired. Quite honestly, I must confess that I've never been so grateful in my life to get fired. When I left Hewlett-Packard, I had a great deal of anxiety and falsely felt as if I had been fired. By contrast, in this instance, I actually was fired and I met it with relief beyond description. I felt grateful that I no longer had to work for these people.

New Lessons in My Living

Since leaving a company where I was dreadfully unhappy, I have learned several lessons that I believe will help me in the future. The difficulties and conflicts that I have had in the past few years have been a means of growth and have given me an opportunity to understand myself better. The years since my firing have given me freedom to do what I wanted to do with my life. These have been years of worry about financial situations, but they have also been years of great reward. Now I have been able to do what I have wanted to do for a long time, engaging in singing, photography and art.

I belong to a men's group that has meant a great deal to me. Each month I look forward to contributing to this group as a way of being with other people and receiving from others. I am living in a world that I appreciate.

Our financial needs have been taken care of, although not quite as well as I might wish for. When I stepped down from the kind of money I was making, I had to learn not to want everything, not to buy everything that I might think I wanted. That was a hard lesson for me to learn. I don't believe that we have thoroughly learned this lesson, but we are trying. Perhaps the economic downturn was good for us because it controlled inflation, making our funds go further. We've been able to live on our retirement money, and we are blessed. My generation had the ethic of work hard, live hard, save your money, invest wisely and you will have what you need in your retirement.

Beginning a New Career

I was anxious about retiring from Hewlett-Packard and eager to leave the short term three-year job. With respect to the latter, my pain exceeded my anxiety. When I left the last job in 2010, I was facing a whole new world and could easily decide to give myself to photography, singing and the things that I enjoyed. I think this decision was driven by the creative, imaginative side of my personality. It seems to me that when I was eager to get another IT job, I was being driven by the carefully structured side of myself, and that didn't work out too well. So maybe something deep in my unconscious was now driving me to explore that other side of my personality – my vocal, artistic, artsy side.

I have mentioned photography as a new vocation. My resolve regarding photography centers around my son, who has been a professional photographer since college. He credits me with his interest in photography and in his choosing it as a vocation. After he chose that world, I asked him if he ever considered that he was entering into a world of low pay, hard work and little affirmation. Perhaps I had more influence on his choice than I imagined, so when I was refocusing my life in 2010, I decided to enter his world and learn from him more about my infatuation with photography. I knew how hard it would be, and I expected very little income from my investment. As I was considering this step, my son confessed that for the first time he made $60,000 last year. Even that amount would be out of the question for a novice like me to earn. Nevertheless, I wanted to take my ability in photography where I had a pure amateur status and try something with him that could be really good.

I knew that this decision was going to be very difficult and provide me with a demanding challenge. It takes a long time to develop a large client base in photography. My goal in joining my son in the world of photography was driven by my desire to share with him an activity that we had in common. One of the first and most important things we have shared was a trip to Las Vegas where we attended a Conference of Professional Photographers.

Those who attended this conference were seeking insight, understanding and methods from those who had made a success in the field. There were dynamic leaders who had a respected status as wedding and portrait photographers from numerous countries. We lived and breathed the atmosphere in this gathering for eight days. We learned about techniques of photography and about the business of photography. We met wonderful, gifted professionals, all of whom were half my age. For a couple of days we studied with a woman who was a professional at making images of weddings. This woman has been my model and mentor ever sense. She is thirty-seven years old, and I'm seventy-one. She has been very successful in building a reputable business. Not only is she my mentor, but she also is my son's mentor. As a consequence of meeting her and seeking to digest her challenges, he has decided to move to Denver, Colorado, where he will be facing a whole new world.

For me to be accepted by these much younger people has been an indescribable, unbelievable gift. I love when my son asks, "How are you holding up? You don't seem to be so old yourself." He also said to me, "I enjoy you and love having you here." So here I am, an old, fledgling photographer being picked up and mentored by my son's contemporaries. Sharing this experience with my son has been one of the high points of my life.

My parents both came from very large families with ten and eleven siblings. That made for a very large, often unhappy extended family, and there was a lot of yelling and screaming almost every day during my younger years. I vowed that I would not be that kind of father to my children. I would hold them, kiss them and let them know they were special to me. I am so proud to watch my grown children share in laughter and care for one another. If one of them needs attention and stroking, the others are there for them. Watching the deep love

133

expressed to my granddaughter by my daughter and now her husband brings joy and tears to my eyes. My relationship with my son ebbs and flows, yet I know I surrounded them with love, and trust they will continue on to live into that legacy.

Another significant blessing has emerged as a result of sharing my passion for photography with my son. As I write this, my dear friend, Steve Hayner, is dying with pancreatic cancer, and I'm deeply moved by his asking me to photograph his presidential portrait which will be hung in the boardroom of Columbia Theological Seminary. His asking me to do this has shown me many aspects of Steve's life and has drawn us closer together, particularly in light of his battle with terminal cancer. As I near the end of this project, I'm deeply humbled and moved when I realize all that went into photographing a friend who is well known around the world. His inviting me to take his picture, recognizing that I had the skills, the background, and the interest has been extraordinarily rewarding. Perhaps this also, in a small way, is part of my legacy, too. This work has been a particular challenge because I am photographing someone whom I know will not be living much longer.

Another notable achievement in photography has grown out of my work with high school seniors and younger kids. In my new calling I have taken a number of photographs of older people. Because of being older myself, I thought perhaps that teenagers and young children were out of my range. Then I realized that working with any age requires the ability to relate to people, no matter how old or young they are. All I need to do with the people I photograph is to help them feel calm, comfortable, and most themselves, and the camera will create living, memorable images. Using my creativity and people skills, I want to expand my learning in this area with the hope that it will become one of the steppingstones to larger and more meaningful areas of service for me.

Looking Ahead

What would I like to achieve over the next ten years? Do I want to pursue dreams and visions for the future, or do I just want to go with the flow? These are age-old questions with which I am dealing once again, this time at the age of seventy-one! My honest answer to these questions is that I am willing to go with the flow and let it take me wherever it will. Living in the flow of my own life means that I will face each day with openness, a welcoming spirit and an excitement about being alive. Perhaps, while living in this flow of life, I will have smaller goals that will sustain my courage, my sense of appreciation for life, and the contribution that I can still make to the world. Who do I want to be when I grow up? What do I want to do with my life? Honestly, I have never fully answered those questions. I have tried to open myself to everything that comes to me, dive into it and participate in it. Perhaps I have often rested too long in one place.

As I consider my age and the brevity of life, I am forced to face a new reality. As I look beyond today, there are things that will come to pass in my life that I would rather not go through. People younger than I am have cancer, and some younger than I have died. I know there are physical pains ahead, there will likely be the loss of friends and there is the possibility of being cast into situations I wish to avoid: ill health, being incapacitated and unable to think or unable to speak. Maybe all those things lie out there ahead of me. Thinking too much about them could bring on depression if I persist in looking at the fearful side of aging. Instead, I try to stay busy and active doing things that are meaningful to me. I continue to try to be more outward-centered and thoughtful of others.

A Word to Retirees

When I was engaged with responsibilities at Hewlett-Packard, I didn't think about retirement, and thus the offer of early retirement came as a shock. As you have read my story of the ups and downs stemming from the issue of retirement, what do you think? How will you face this major change in life? Preparing for retirement is a difficult and complicated issue.

My suggestion in preparing for this event is that you take stock of yourself. Recognize the things that are worthwhile and lovable in your life. Think about how you might help someone who is struggling with life decisions. Look for small ways you can help a fellow traveler. As we have heard many times, "Leave the world a little better place than it was when you came into it."

Perhaps my life has been exactly what it was meant to be – nothing more, nothing less. It has been my life, and I am grateful for all that I have learned in living it.

17. My Life Transitions Explored

"I think this is a transition from a life of becoming to a life more focused on being; one of existence as a "human being," not a "human doing."

When I was invited to write my story for this book, of course I said, "Yes." It is always a great honor to be asked to contribute in this way, and doubly so when the request comes from someone I admire.

After I had committed myself, this project sounded especially interesting to me: exploring life transitions. The shifts in perspective are occurring when we ask questions such as: What signals transition? What helps us move through a transition? What continues and what changes? The big changes are birth and death.

While I was honored to be invited to contribute, I found myself continuing to put this project aside. I reflected and realized I was doing so not just out of procrastination and distraction, but because doing justice to the topic required a deep examination of which transitions I would explore, and this was proving difficult. In fact, I eventually realized the first question for me to explore was not, "what transitions?" but rather, "from what perspective?"

The most obvious and natural seemed to be my life history. With little memory of childhood, especially early childhood, I can only start the story with the increasingly strong memories that begin with the transition through puberty, and include leaving home to go to college; entering into my first sexual relationships; moving into the workforce when I got my first real job and became, in a traditional sense, independent; emigrating to the USA; falling in love and getting married; having children; and the whole series of career and family evolutions that followed from there.

But I realized that this simple chronology of growing up is not very interesting either to me or, I am sure, to others; nor does it allow me to meaningfully explore the deeper questions of transition as I understood the question.

So I started thinking about different categories of transition, and after a while placed them into two broad categories. On the one hand there are transitions born of material and mental change: these are about physical growth; hormonal change; learning about and moving through the world. They are transitions of power and strength and wealth; transitions of responsibility and role. They are the most obvious transitions (and the ones that tend to show up in a traditional chronological life story), but they are not ones I think of as bearing on the real question.

The other category I see as much more important and relevant: these are the transitions through quality of consciousness; the cultivation of awareness and of self-reflection; the shifts in quality of being. In a sense, the former transitions represent our journey in the outside world, and the latter our journey through the inner world.

From this standpoint the first two-thirds of my life hold little interest: I was intellectually gifted and, by honing and concentrating on this ability, I was very successful: I passed many difficult exams, was hired into challenging jobs; and achieved promotions, pay increases and ever higher levels of responsibility. I was attractive and popular and experienced the natural emotions of family love which bound me closely to my family of birth and later to my wife and children. But I did all of this with very little real self-awareness. Worse, I lacked even the level of awareness to realize its absence, to the extent that fifteen years ago I would have confidently asserted I had full consciousness and self-awareness, and I would have been completely incapable of seeing what I am now talking about.

Beginnings

I led most of my life blind to spirituality, and it has been only in the last fifteen years that I have had the opportunity to experience the kind of growth that I think is called for in the question of life transitions. So my story of transitions really begins fifteen years ago when I was already married and a father and at the height of a successful corporate career.

But of course reality is not as convenient as that, for internal and external journeys don't separate neatly in this simplistic manner. With deeper thinking, I believe the place to begin this story is with my transition into marriage.

Falling in love and dating and spending time with my first wife will always be one of the most incredible and wonderful periods in my life. The early years of our marriage – including an extraordinary honeymoon in Ecuador – were among the happiest times I have known and could imagine. I will cherish many memories of this time until my dying day: arriving back at our small apartment after a magical two-week honeymoon in Ecuador, putting on an Andean music cassette tape we had bought, and dancing in the midst of our unpacked luggage; driving from Charlotte to our new home, Atlanta, in a small car full of bags, boxes, a small dog, and a beta fish; and a stunning and incredibly sexy wife meeting me in a summer frock and pumps when I returned from my first international business trip. This truly was a major transition in my life. But what was it about?

Transitions are rarely, if ever, visible from inside, from their own time and place. Looking back, I think this one was about making an absolute commitment. I had fallen in love and sensed I wanted to spend the rest of my life with one special woman– though telling her this, asking her to marry me, and walking into the church on the day of our marriage were among the most difficult things I've ever done. So I think this transition was about deeply committing to and connecting with another person. I think this was a move toward accepting responsibility and surrendering some level of ego. In a very real sense it was the transition from childhood to adulthood. It was accompanied by the decision that I would stay in the US (which until that time had been uncertain), and by leaving my parents and my family of birth for another family (over the years my wife's family became very dear to me). The transitions that followed – buying a home, having children, earning a living, building a life together – were not so much transitions in themselves but increments to the big one I had already undertaken. Yes, being present at the birth of my children; feeding them and changing their diapers; watching the world anew through their eyes – all of these were incredible times of my life, but they were incremental steps in a natural and inevitable continuum that began with my proposal to my first wife.

What signaled this transition? What continued and what changed?

Yes, there was certainly a surrender of self in this deep commitment to another soul, and that is an important part of the answer. But ironically I think that much of this move into intimate companionship was also about moving into independence. It was about finally being ready to grow up and leave my family of origin. It was a first faltering move to discovering who I really am, and learning that real independence cannot exist without real interconnectedness, that they are actually just opposing sides of the same story. From that standpoint the nervousness that was so profound the presiding priest cut the service short makes sense to me now. At a deep, subconscious level I knew the magnitude of this change and it was terrifying – but also necessary. The move to independence, to autonomy, to responsibility is one that requires us to leave much behind, but at the same time makes us more available, more open, more loving not just to that into which we move, but towards that which is left behind. It's too early in the story to look at what remains, but this is a real stepping stone in the larger arc of my life's spiritual journey.

Meditation

My first move into what I now see as the stage of my life more interesting to this story came out of a time of emotional crisis and a level of awakening to the limited perspective I had of my life. It's easy to see, looking back, that I craved stimulation, but this was not visible to me at the time. I lived on the thrill of my career; on managing my money and the excitement of spending it on "stuff" and experiences; on vicarious living through books, movies and computer games; and of course stoking my addictive furnace with alcohol and cigarettes. All of this activity kept my adrenalin levels and blood pressure high. I led a life addicted simultaneously to excitement and the thrills of career and success, coupled with the drugs of escape and release.

But along the way I had a glimpse that I was missing what really matters in life, that things were not quite what they seemed. I was a mergers and acquisitions executive for BellSouth and had been out of town for weeks on end putting together a large and complicated deal. I came back through Atlanta for just a couple of days before leaving again to resurrect a couple of deals in Latin America that I had put on hold. Passing through the living room on one of those mornings, my two-year-old son ran up to the father he had not seen for several weeks, called out "Daddy," and grabbed my leg. But I needed to leave, so I shook him off and hurried out the door. I put this experience aside and flew to Latin America, but I believe my son's cry was the bolt of lightning that lit a spark deep inside me which started to smolder.

The transformational story I remember has been reinforced by retelling, and realistically it probably didn't happen quite this way. But equally it was probably closer to this than I would like, and I have no doubt that if I could go back and watch myself that morning, I would cringe. Certainly this story captures the emotional impact of this incident which so profoundly affected me.

But even with that emotional impact, had circumstances not conspired to help me, I could easily have re-immersed myself in the thrill of the deal world and let the ember go out.

Within a year of this incident the Internet bubble burst, the Telecom market collapsed, and my exciting life changed dramatically. The aftershock of the market collapse continued for several more years through a series of headline corporate scandals and bankruptcies (including WorldCom), but my fast track career in Telecom had hit a wall. I threw myself wholeheartedly at the next wave of work, but it was theoretical and office-bound and not the same. I yearned for the thrill of the hunt that the corporate big game hunters enjoy, a thrill that would not return. So I filled the void with my other addictions, one of which was always looking for a new thrill. A passing whim led me to opera and classical music, then into a course of study that took me back to listening to medieval Christian masses. Through this exploration something wonderful and entirely unexpected happened.

The religious awe and devotion of composers such as Guillaume de Machaut, Palestrina, Josquin des Prez, and Johann Sebastian Bach reached down over the centuries and spoke to me through their music. In doing so, they started to fan the ember that was still smoldering inside me: I experienced awe and faith that I did not understand and could not explain. Recognizing its source, I was drawn into reading about ancient Christianity. And that, in turn, led me into a study of comparative religions, and to learning about the contemplative practices that reside within all the major world religions.

I had found a new addiction: I read extensively about different religions and was enthralled by the experiences described by mystics in all of the faiths. But this addiction, rather than being just another thrill, another distraction, was a gentle fan, ever warming the ember inside me.

One day the ember burst spontaneously into flame. On that day I determined to try meditating.

I was very self-conscious and didn't tell anyone – even my wife– what I planned to do. I was about to dabble in some occult and dangerous dark art, a craft akin to painting a pentagram in blood on the floor, and I was afraid. But somehow the call was too strong and overcame my inhibitions. One Sunday afternoon, when my family was out, I lay down on the couch, closed my eyes, and meditated for the first time. I performed a Vipassana-style meditation on the body, beginning with close examination of the hair, then the top of the head, moving awareness slowly down the body and exiting through the toes.

When I opened my eyes and sat up after fifteen minutes, I felt clear and fresh. The room was bright and clean and vibrant with color and life. As was my habit at that time, I went out onto the deck to reflect on what had transpired over a cigarette. But I was conscious of my actions in a way I had never been before. My fingers felt fat and clumsy as they reached awkwardly into the packet; the white cylinder they pulled out was the size of a tree trunk and filled with intoxicant and tar. Why was I putting this stuff into my lungs, into my blood? Why did my body need this stimulation? I had just examined my life-giving lungs, whose delicate absorptive tissue permitting gaseous exchange gives life, but was now going to abuse them as a means to excite the body. How could I inhale a known carcinogen, a sea of tar; how could I subject my body to this? Worse, how could I impose this voluntary destructive act on the body of my children's father, knowing that it would cause them great pain and anguish through a premature and painful death?

My first experience of meditation had triggered my first experience of mindfulness. Its power and richness faded, but the awakening into mindfulness would not go away. Over the next few years, periods of extensive daily meditation alternated with periods when I decided I "got it" and stopped meditating. But through it all a level of awareness of what I was doing kept pulling me back. It was only weeks before I would quit smoking, just a couple of years before I quit drinking, and just five years before I would make a major career transition. My meditation led quickly to a frantic burst of writing that settled into the more routine work I do today; to me returning to playing the piano that I had quit as a kid; and to spending more time at home and concentrating more of my energy on my family.

Like the other transitions in my life, this had a long buildup to a critical event from which I could never return, and a long period of adjustment after the transition. In this case the suppressed response to my son grabbing my leg led me into an exploration that would lead to the awakening, through meditation, of the mindfulness experience and practice that would completely change the rest of my life.

Interfaith and Leaving My Zen Teacher

I think of this next major transition in my life as leaving my Zen teacher, but in reality it was about a lot more than that. And it grew out of my meditation practice.

For two or so years after my first experience, I meditated alone in my home. But as my experiences became more intense and as I became more committed to the practice, I came to the conclusion that I needed a teacher. This is what the books said, and their advice resonated with my experience. So I went looking. I searched the Internet and my books and I wrote letters to teachers. I also visited local practitioners in Atlanta, though more out of desperation than hope, because I hadn't seen much in my search that would fit my need. But my letters came up empty, and I didn't believe myself able to travel in this search, so more by convenience and laziness than anything else, I found myself regularly attending a local Zen Center and taking on its abbot as my spiritual guide, as my teacher.

Over a ten-year period I came to treasure not just my teacher, but also the community. As I understand it, Zen in Japan is largely a congregational faith, much like regular Christianity in the US, but for many of us in the West it is different: it does not mean a physical place for short weekly services or a forum to recognize life events, but rather symbolizes a serious, time-consuming commitment to a dedicated course of study and meditation and to the cultivation of mindfulness. The community I joined had many members as passionately engaged in cultivating their spiritual path as I was my own. I not only had rich conversations with them, but also found great support in the strength of their practice. And of course I derived great benefit from my relationship with the teacher. As a result of my own commitment to the community and some advancement in my understanding, I was offered increasing levels of leadership and responsibility and was ordained a priest.

Things Start to Go Wrong

A couple of rather abrupt and ugly incidents woke me up to see that friends of mine in the community were having real difficulties with the teacher – what I can only describe as bullying, behavior by the teacher directed at controlling the students in ways hurtful to them. I also began to see he was directing the organization towards his personal financial goals. Compelled to look at this for the first time while deciding what to do, I slowly realized that I too was being bullied.

The misbehavior I experienced is what I generally describe as "small church stuff"; it is the inevitable consequence of a faith leader acting without peer support, without adequate income, and with no real accountability to a board or organizational body. Unfortunately this kind of situation is common in Western incarnations of many Eastern faith traditions, including Zen Buddhism. With the benefit of time and emotional distance I now see that in addition to being bullied, I had "drunk the Kool-Aid" in a couple of ways. First, I had come to accept a role supporting my teacher's personal goals at the expense of the community, thereby enabling his behavior and beliefs; and second, I had accepted Zen Buddhism as the one true faith. In short, I had lost sight of my original goal of cultivating wisdom and compassion.

But the self is far smarter than we give it credit for being. I'm pretty sure that deep inside me something was holding on to this goal. This something latched on when I first experienced interfaith and would not let go. My ability to locate things precisely in space and time is long gone, but I remember enough to know that my first exposure to interfaith was somewhere in my last few years with this Zen group, and that I was hooked. It was not clear for the longest time what this was really about, but it catalyzed a major change in direction in my life, one that likely woke me up to the suffering of my friends at the Zen Center and gave me the strength and urgency to leave.

I had undertaken the path of spirituality to examine and deal with my internal demons. I focused first on my alcoholism, and from there moved into my over-commitment to work, my poor relationships with family, and my lack of friends outside work. Zen became a place where I cultivated awareness of my obsessive, compulsive and neurotic existence and in which this started to evanesce. It was a wonderful and necessary experience for me, but as I continued the practice, in a sense I started losing connection with the world. Interfaith was a much needed breath of connection for me. It resonated with my earlier reading that the same depth of experience and connection that I found in my Zen practice and experience was available in other faiths. While I already knew this intellectually, experiencing it changed my life. It started to shift me from an internally focused practice to one that equally looked externally. Sure, doing this is part of the teaching of Zen, but I needed the interfaith experience and community to help me see it.

With my interfaith experience I began to engage in more intimate relationships with others, and in doing so I came to recognize not so much the "small church stuff" – though that was very important – but the need for me to move out into a larger world, a larger realm of life.

Therapy and Divorce

Spiritual practice cultivates awareness. Through that come healing, reduction of anxiety, and naturally making oneself more useful in the world. But spiritual practice also has a dark side and can breed a certain arrogance. It was thus for me. This arrogance had made me blind to the traps I was falling into within my Zen community, blind to failures in my marriage and my relationships with family, blind to the extent of my ignorance, and blind to seeing that I was really still the same person I had always been.

I was not just blind to difficulties in marriage, but lacked the knowledge and insight to even recognize them when they were presented. I lacked the self-awareness to recognize my contribution to the problems and the humility to really work on healing them. Thus, for a decade our marriage stagnated without my realizing it. This blurring of what had been such a wonderful relationship in its beginning may seem strange. Little by little I began to see that we were growing apart, and I didn't know all the reasons. I suspect that the intensity of my search pushed me more deeply into myself and farther from my wife because she was not on the same journey.

My wife had a much greater realization of this than I did, though of course she was also contributing to the growing distance between us. But it was her realization that opened up a conversation about our problems, and we entered marriage therapy.

With hindsight a lot of what I was learning was about the extent to which a successful marriage requires ongoing work by both partners on the relationship itself to maintain intimacy, romance, and regular connection. My wife and I had neglected this work for many years. As a result we had simply allowed ourselves to grow so far apart that when I wanted to reconnect, there was a huge gap between us.

This was a process that lasted several years and I learned a lot, though while it was happening I did not realize much of what I was learning. And this was running in parallel with my spiritual development, as a result of which I was increasingly bumping into major blockages around my immaturity in sexual relationships and around my poor relationship with my life partner. I did not really know what these were about, but I did know they were causing me increasing levels of trauma. At one point I had been out of town for a few days and could not bring myself to return home to what felt like the loneliest place in the world; and almost a year later I had a couple of other similar events. I think, with hindsight, that I was in a dark emotional spiral and headed to a meltdown that would result in the collapse of my business and maybe even a nervous breakdown. I was miserable, getting worse, and could see no way out.

Finally, with desperation and urgency, I brought up in our marriage therapy session that I needed a safe place of my own. I said that while I had, and still have, a great affection for our therapist, private sessions with him were simply not working for me. I had asked this before but been pushed back; this time, though, against my wife's objections, our therapist agreed and gave me a referral.

Shortly after I started working with my own therapist, my wife shared her concern that a marriage partner who starts an independent course of counseling usually leaves the marriage. I did not see things that way; I felt myself still committed to the process, and pushed to change marriage therapists, but I now realize my wife was right.

Actually I've had this conversation more recently with my therapist, and she agreed with my wife, too. She added that in my particular case she realized very soon after I walked into her office that I was done with the marriage, but had not allowed myself to see it. She also recognized that for all my mindfulness and meditation practice, I had neither looked very deeply into why I was who I was, nor cultivated skills for dealing with my relationships. Our early work took me back into my childhood, into my relationships with my parents and into the experiences that had formed my ego and identity.

I learned fairly quickly while working with Allie that meditation does not naturally deal with the dark places from our childhood, nor equip us with the sensitivity to engage compassionately in difficult conversations. It does, however, develop a softness and openness such that the work of therapy, once engaged, can move very fast. So Allie took me deep into places in myself that I had long forgotten, and I found myself weeping in her office out of sadness for my mother. She helped me find the small child hidden inside me that was yearning for the relationship with his father that he had always been denied.

I realized with Allie that I did not need to "fix" things; rather, I had to use the techniques I had cultivated in my spiritual practice to explore different parts of myself; and I needed to learn a whole new way of relating to people, a way of listening and of curiosity and of soft starts.

I also learned more about the inseparability of mind and body. I thought I understood this from my Zen practice, but I had done so more intellectually than experientially. With Allie I physically located the suppressed child inside (hiding in my lower belly, slightly off center to the left); I physically experienced holding my stress in my shoulders; and I learned that daily, strenuous exercise changed my mental energy and sense of well-being. It took only a few months of personal therapy to develop a level of self-awareness and self-confidence to be ready to move on with life. I told my wife that I was leaving our marriage and a business partner that I was leaving our relationship, too. I had left my Zen teacher six months before starting therapy with Allie, a leaving associated with this same phase of my life. In a real sense, though, I had not moved on, and my work in therapy allowed me to do so.

As with so much in my life, I had let my problems and failures accumulate to the point that I was about to fail catastrophically before dealing with them. This time I was able to do so from a place of insight and understanding of who I am and what I also need. Allie Caffyn has been one of the most powerful and beautiful forces in my life, and the work she took me through allowed me to see clearly the childhood conditioning that continued to lead me into sowing my relationships with the seeds of failure. Her teachings allowed me not just to leave behind failed relationships and the hold their traumas had on me, but also the habits that would have led me to repeat them. She helped me develop skills to do a much better job of relationships as I move forward in my life.

Arriving

While reflecting and writing about the transitions so far, I have been thinking of them as transitions of leaving; approaching this last transition, though, I see it as one of arrival. But that is because I can't help writing from a particular perspective, the perspective of "here I am, now I am." I will probably always look at my life, my transitions, from the standpoint of leaving the past and arriving in the present. Perhaps from a larger perspective the transition I am living right now is actually not different from the others, but from within I think it must have the flavor of arriving. So I will write of it as such.

I also choose to write of it as "arriving" because I think it has a different flavor. It feels as if I am moving into who I am and who I was meant to be. I recognize, though, that may also be a conceit, and that in a sense I am always and have always been who I am or was and who I am or was meant to be at any particular time.

Either way, the transitions I have described, although spread over several years, have been very disruptive to my life and left it very much still in flux. I feel I have entered a period of settling in, of making my new home. This period of settling in sounds less dramatic, maybe not even a real transition, but I think it is profoundly important for me and think it is directly relevant to this story. There is a lot going on in this transition, which is not just a transition of arriving, but in a sense it is the bridge to the rest of my life, and I see a very different future for myself than I did even two years ago.

During my period of leaving I took on considerable obligations. I co-founded a Buddhist group and assumed the responsibility of being one of its spiritual and organizational leaders; I took on leadership positions in many interfaith organizations and communities; I assumed significant financial obligations for alimony, child support, and college fees for my kids; I had to put a lot of work into engaging with my kids and building a new relationship with them; and changes in my business life left me with much to do around rebuilding my brand and sources of income.

But through all of this, I have found this period to be a time of profound freedom. I come home at night to my own home, free from the anxiety of sharing space with a wife I didn't know how to approach or how to be with. I am free of a vision of a future I didn't know or understand, a future of heavy but unarticulated and unplanned obligations. I am freed of this future I now realize I didn't want and found scary.

I am free to hope, free to enjoy and free to be happy.

Freedom to enjoy means freedom to explore, freedom to start anew. Among other things this has allowed me to move into my spiritual journey in new ways. A blog grew out of my interfaith journey, and it quickly moved from an outlet for my writing to becoming a passion and a large part of how I identify myself. This work has broadened to include lectures, a podcast, and a sense that it might actually be important in a way I don't quite understand. A large part of my being has shifted from that of a disciple bound to obey in a particular faith tradition into a free spirit, living, practicing, and speaking about my own personal faith journey and faith experiences in ways that connect with a broader group of people.

As I experimented in my spiritual practice, I visited many sacred spaces, observed Ramadan and the Jewish High Holidays, and explored the teachings of sages of many traditions, among them Nisargadatta, a name I had heard occasionally in my Buddhist group. Reading a book of his conversations has completely changed my life.

Nisargadatta, who died in 1981, is a realized being out of the Hindu tradition. He lived a modest life in India and wrote nothing, though many of his talks were recorded and published by his disciples. His teachings are probably not deeper than those of others, but his voice works for me. Strangely, though I experience him only in his transcribed conversations, I connect deeply with him in a way that is beyond words – as well as apparently beyond death! His picture on my office credenza is a reminder every day of his presence in my life, and his voice, like those of J.S. Bach and Josquin des Prez, brings his wisdom down over the years to profoundly influence and affect me.

In addition to deepening my relationships with my kids, learning to be present with them and live for them in ways I could not have imagined a few years ago, I have also moved into an incredible and profoundly intimate relationship with a woman I originally met through my Buddhist practices. We have developed a level of trust in each other and an ability to share intimacy and to work on our relationship that is brand new to me and is not only an amazing and wonderful experience in itself, but a way of being that is affecting my whole life.

I don't think I can truly know what the current transition is really about while I am in it, both because I can have no objective perspective of it, and because I have no idea where it is going, but I think I have a good guess.

I think this is a transition from a life of becoming to a life more focused on being; one of existence as a "human being," not a "human doing." In moving my energy from "doing" to "being," I am much more present with those I love and care for, including my own self. As my life and the teachings I am imbibing move me incrementally into a world of being, I am shedding a lot of what I thought was important to me: the formal labels of faith; the sense of ego in my livelihood; a desire to be recognized as successful or important; and even a lot of my possessions, which I am simply giving away.

This transition has, in a sense, only just begun, but in another sense it has always been there. It is the transition of surrender and relinquishing in which I am simultaneously gaining so much, a transition that began with my first marriage and has been deepening ever since. It is a transition that will continue until all that is left is my deepest self, pure being, unconditional love.

18. Dealing with Alzheimer's

*"With a smile and a soft touch, I welcome any
recognition, nice words and gentleness he offers."*

The depth of love that I have for my husband, Arthur, has become the
depth of my sorrow and grief. So my story of being his caregiver begins
as I also explore the depth of my grief. In 2009 he was diagnosed with
Mild Cognitive Impairment (MCI). His memory loss had begun two or
three years earlier. The diagnosis of Alzheimer's came in 2010, though
he actually had the beginning several years previously. This disease has
changed my life in every respect – my marriage, my vocation and my
meaning in life.

Assistance in Functioning

During the early days of Arthur's disease, I learned to deal with the
various changes that his memory loss brought on; it disrupted every
aspect of his daily life. He couldn't remember anything. I began
leaving reminder notes of his appointments; I helped him with names
of people he had known for years. I patiently answered questions that
he asked over and over. I started reminding him of the day of the week
and the year and the time of day. I took over bill payments when he no
longer remembered to pay them. All the things that I had counted on
him to do all of our marriage, I now had to assume responsibility for
them.

Other very basic activities, which had always been a part of his
life, I had to assist him with. I helped him with card playing that he
had done his entire life. I helped him find the right words to express
his thoughts, and I learned that I needed to just go along with him
when he thought people were stealing his things. Along with these
adjustments I also learned ways to soothe him when he became angry
or irritable. I started diverting his attention away from his frustration
when he became confused. I began using fewer words to communicate

because he seemed to follow better when I did so. To further assist his understanding, I stopped asking him to think about more than one thing at a time. It seemed to help his adjustment when I made sure that the atmosphere in our home was calm and quiet. When I wanted him to get my message, I held his hands and had him look at me when I spoke to him. He seemed to settle down when we spent lots of time dancing to soft music or sitting quietly on the sofa, watching a TV show, hugging and kissing each other. We took walks with our dog, Molly, and I sang songs to him that he had always liked to hear. All of these activities that I initiated were aimed at making life easier for my husband and creating an environment that would help him feel secure.

Preserving Independence

As time passed, Arthur's symptoms worsened. It became obvious to me that I had to find new ways to ease the 24/7 task of caring for him. He would forget to eat and then begin telling me how hungry he was. I started preparing small amounts of different foodstuffs and kept them in the refrigerator so he could help himself when he felt the least bit hungry. I very much wanted to allow him to feel independent. For example, he wanted to write checks to pay bills. I went along with his desire and if he incorrectly filled in some checks, I just re-wrote them. From my phenomenal Alzheimer's support group family, I learned how to deal with the idiosyncrasies that my husband began to display. I not only accepted but encouraged him to do everything for himself even if it was not exactly appropriate, like wearing two or three pairs of socks or two undershirts or two dress shirts and two sweaters. Sometimes he wore all these on top of each other. If he asked for my help, I responded. He always said, "Thank you," and he still does.

An Appropriate Home

Today, Arthur's home is the memory care section of Insignia in Atlanta, Georgia. When he came to the stage where he began getting up in the middle of the night, getting confused about where he was or where he was going, he fell and I couldn't pick him up. By this time, he had forgotten everything he ever knew about hygiene, dressing, eating with proper utensils, courtesy and self-control. His words were often scrambled, particularly when he was irritated, which was often.

His language became abusive, as did his behavior. I eventually got the strength to let go of the anger and the hurt I felt when he'd hit me or make unkind remarks. I struggled with my conscience and cried all the time about the decision that I had to make, and I remained constantly exhausted. My head told me I had to take him somewhere to live; my heart simply wouldn't allow me to do it. I hired a Certified Nursing Assistant (CNA) who came for a few hours five days a week. While I had this additional help, I visited several facilities. I prepared a list of forty questions, which amazed every director I spoke to; the list now has grown to fifty. These questions are currently being used by members of my support group as well as by the center that cares for my husband. Here are some of the basic questions I thought necessary to ask every facility director.

1. What would be your first question if you were seeking a facility for your loved one? Gives you an idea about attitude and catches listener's attention.
2. How old is the facility?
3. How many residents in assisted living/memory care?
4. What is the cost of room/care in assisted living/memory care?
5. Ratio of staff to residents in assisted living/memory care day and night?
6. Is this facility privately owned, and if so, by whom?
7. If not privately owned, who is the parent company and how many facilities do they own? Any others in the Atlanta area?
8. Is this a profit or nonprofit facility?
9. How long has present owner owned the facility?
10. Can you give me a breakdown of staff members like Registered Nurses, CNAs, Physical/Occupational Therapists, Activities Director, and any other staff members who have contact with the residents?
11. What is the weekly housekeeping program for assisted living/ memory care?
12. What kind of security is provided for assisted living/memory care?
13. How do you handle outside visitation in assisted living/memory care, i.e., can anyone walk in and see a resident? What if someone

comes in and wants to take resident out for lunch, etc. How is this arranged? Do you want a list of regular visitors?

14. Do you have respite care? How much does it cost?

15. How do you handle emergencies?

16. What items do I need to provide for a room/bathroom? Do you provide anything for the rooms? Do you have a list of items I am responsible for?

17. What are some of the in-house programs you provide? Exercise? Lectures? Games? Entertainment? Special holiday events?

18. What are some of the outside activities you do and how often?

19. Are all residents (assisted living & memory care) involved in all indoor and outdoor activities if they are capable and have a desire to join in?

20. What personal services are provided for the residents? Is there a list of services and costs?

21. Are all residents (assisted living and memory care), if able, entitled to avail themselves of all services?

22. Can I expect a cost increase every year and approximately how much?

23. If my loved one has special dietary do's or don'ts, can you accommodate that?

24. Can visitors join residents for lunch and dinner? What is the cost?

25. Can you provide transportation for appointments (medical/dental, etc.) if needed?

26. What is the cost of this service?

27. Can I pay the monthly cost with a credit card or direct payment from a financial institution (bank, brokerage house, etc.)?

28. How do you handle administering meds to the residents?

29. Is there a medically certified person on the premises at all times?

Further Natural Process

I visit Arthur regularly, but I have asked the staff not to resuscitate him if he begins to slip away. He is now off all medications except those that lessen his anxiety or help him sleep or avoid a stroke. After having lived at Insignia for six months, his anxiety and irritable behavior have lessened. He mostly responds positively to those Certified Nursing

Assistants who truly care about his quality of life. He is still mobile, in good health and he eats well. We have meaningful times together: we listen to music, look at recent pictures and those taken long ago, take walks, hold hands, embrace and kiss. We frequently exchange "I love you" between the two of us and lots of "thank you, sweetheart." He no longer expresses emotion or passion, sadness or anger. With a smile and a soft touch, I welcome any recognition, nice words and gentleness he offers. I take him outside the memory care unit for haircuts, manicures and pedicures. He sits in the rear of the car for protection where I buckle him up and safety lock the doors and the windows.

My Commitment

During the years I have been caregiver to Arthur, I have concluded that my life is totally dedicated to working with and for the Alzheimer's community, personally with my husband, family and friends, and reaching out into my community and beyond. My niece and I are presently working on a website where I will be able to reach out to others with my writing about the Alzheimer's journey. I want to establish a place from which I can answer questions and give support to those who are new to the journey. I now have the knowledge to help those who do not know how to deal with loved ones in the various stages of the disease – looking for day care facilities, finding an appropriate doctor, attorney, or financial adviser. Because my husband is a Veteran of Foreign Wars, I know what to expect from the Veterans Administration with respect to administering meds, seeing doctors, residential living, nursing homes, financial assistance, etc.

I am now involved with several residents who live in the same memory care unit as my husband. We have bonded to the extent that they recognize and give me a smile when I visit. When we meet, we hug, kiss, and chat. My acting skills allow me to get them smiling or laughing on most occasions. I dance and sing and can sometimes get them to clap their hands. Once in a while, I join everyone at the center for dinner. The residents are joyful when I bring our dog Molly for a visit.

I strongly advocate for adult day care centers. Working with the Weinstein Adult Day Care Center showed me how every resident has the need to feel important and useful. I urge everyone that I counsel to consider keeping their loved one at home as long as possible, taking him or her to an adult day care center that fosters feelings of self-enrichment, self-reliance and self-esteem. When I visit the Center, my heart swells when I see how almost every person is engaged in an individual project or a community project. I rejoice when I sense their enjoyment and interest. Truly, it was a sad day when my husband would no longer get out of bed to go to the Center. We still encourage him and, on occasion, he will go to the Center where he has a meaningful time. Before he moved into Insignia, we told him he had to get up and go to work. He even got a pay check. He loved that idea and did, indeed, perform simple tasks at the Center.

At the request of Georgia Gunter, the Director of the Weinstein Center, I met with the Health Committee members of the Georgia Legislature in January 2014. I asked the committee members and others like myself attending the session, how many of them knew of someone who had Alzheimer's? Ninety percent of the entire room raised their hands. I then asked them if they would consider putting a loved one into an unlicensed adult day care center. The bill to require centers to be licensed had been sitting around since 2004. Fortunately, it passed both houses and was signed into law by the Governor at the end of the 2014 session. A year has passed since I met with the committee and the elected officials. In recent days I have been asked to review a video aimed at educating caregivers about Alzheimer's and teaching them how to respond to their loved ones at the various stages of the disease. The owners of the video are hoping to market this instructional product in order to raise funds to cover organizational expenses.

Grief Remains, but Love Goes On

The grief is always present, but it softens each day as I realize the joy that I share with Arthur on those occasions when I am with him and he is with me, awake and aware and engaged with me; talking about who knows what, touching, kissing, hugging, dancing, softly singing and feeling the love we know we have for one another in the particular moment. Arthur says, "You do know I love you very much." I echo his words as my unseen tears are masked by my smile. "I love you too, my sweetheart."

The depth of my love for my precious husband has deepened; the sorrow has lessened, thanks to so many who have blessed me with love and encouragement. When I write about the depth of my love becoming the depth of my sorrow, I intend to express this message: if one is gifted to feel the zenith of joy (love), one will also experience the nadir of sadness (grief or sorrow), but this too can be a gift. I believe that one has to equal the other in order to feel the fullness of the total experience. I am blessed by having both in my life.

THE JOURNEY CONTINUES.

19. Confessions of an Octogenarian

"If we make the transition to old age with a warm acceptance of our true self, it leads to a wonderful freedom."

When I was sixteen years old, I wondered what it would be like to be eighty. After only a few steps into my ninth decade, I can report first-hand on the wonderings of that teenage kid. To begin with, living in the ninth decade means that I have to deal with worn-out body parts. Some of the parts can be repaired; others need to be replaced. I think I can get a little more mileage with the new parts. Some body parts don't wear out, they just act out. Take atrial fibrillation, for example; one's heart keeps speeding up until it runs away. Medication helps keep the electrical impulses under control. I have lived with an irregular heartbeat for more than twenty years. I have often wondered if this ticker inside of me will be the door through which I walk into the next life.

I've had a couple of body parts replaced – two bionic hips that set off the buzzer at the airport every time I pass through the metal detector, and two new lenses in my eyes that help me read signs at a distance. The replacements have made life more interesting.

I've been through different stages of hearing loss. First, the stage of questioning: "What did you say?" There are numerous variations on this theme – "Would you say that again? Would you repeat that, please? Holler!" To alleviate the embarrassment of requesting repeated performances, I finally got hearing aids, sat with my back to the wall in restaurants and learned to nod and smile when I had no idea what people were saying.

At age sixty I wondered why old people wobbled when they walked. I now know. They wobble because they lack a sense of balance and fear that they will fall on their face if they rush too fast. If a person wobbles too much, it can lead to a fall – a fall going to the bathroom at night, going up steps, failing to step high enough to make the curb. At eighty,

I began to walk like an old man and one day when I was pondering this behavior, I said to myself, "I'm not like an old man, I am an old man."

The digestive system and the necessity for elimination and urination seem to be confused about their functions. During my first decades, everything worked fine. When I did have some slight problem, a laxative or an antibiotic provided a remedy. Adding more fiber or roughage in my diet doesn't work. Taking a diuretic interrupts sleep, though it may be keeping one alive.

Perhaps one might consider these changes to be among the greatest that a person can suffer, but I don't think so. I think that the loss of love-making is a greater problem. For over forty years the gift of sex has been important to me and to our marriage, and the passionate feelings, the looks, and touches nurture the relationship and make it deeply fulfilling.

To help me deal with changes I was experiencing, one day I had lunch with a Hindu physician who had openly talked about becoming celibate in his later years. During the lunch I asked him about his celibate experience, and he related how Hindu men look at sex in three stages; the first twenty or twenty-five years they are celibate until they are married; for the next four decades they enjoy and appreciate sex; at some point past sixty, they return to celibacy. During this period they concentrate on their relation with God and preparation for dying. After this conversation, I decided to accept my physical and emotional losses as opportunities for personal growth.

I have not been in this struggle alone. My wife has been a supportive companion. I could not ask for deeper understanding, warmer encouragement and the dependable stability that I have received from her.

Along with the losses the journey enters new levels of awareness that come with aging. Gone is the struggle to be noted, praised or elevated for one's achievements. I spent over sixty years seeking human approval and adulation; that achievement no longer propels me. Instead of the "me" focus, I find a greater interest in others. How can I help them use their gifts? What wisdom can I share? What can I offer others that will enrich their lives? This sharing takes the form of friendships, writing and helping others write, being sensitive to people who need a word of encouragement or material help. This outward focus brings a new depth of meaning to life.

Whereas most of my life has been focused on doing, this emphasis seems to be shifting. I've spent much of my life creating a company, dreaming into existence programs and courses. I have spent many hours writing books, pamphlets and articles. Doing! Now I don't have the energy to keep such a harried pace; now I have more time to listen, to reflect on my life and my present awareness. I give some time wondering about my life, what it has meant, why I am here. I'm thankful for the opportunities that I've had to see the world, to work in many different settings and to know a variety of people and share both in their joys and sorrows, their triumphs and pain.

If we make the transition to old age with a warm acceptance of our true self, it leads to a wonderful freedom. In old age I experience freedom from the need to achieve, to impress and to acquire more things. The recognition that I have enough of everything necessary for my life pervades my consciousness. This freedom also has theological dimensions. Early on I had a certain kind of paralysis that blocked my open view of the truth. Through the graciousness of God, I began to see a much larger world and experience an expanded consciousness of the core of my soul. I saw new implications of my faith, and a certitude deepened around my beliefs. By some gift of sight, I began to see the deeper meaning of theological concepts, the reality of a world that is still being created and the vision of a whole, unified humanity. Thankfully, I began to see the validity of faith in other religions. My interest became more loving toward those who were different, instead of wanting to convert them. What a joy to know the freedom of being part of God's whole world.

This place of aging has brought with it an expectancy and hope for the next stage of being. From time to time I experience brief glimpses of the future that produce a scintillating sense of hope and anticipation.

Age is deepened and enriched through the gift of memories – memories of earlier times, of relationships developed, of a hand larger than my own guiding my life, the gift of family, children and grandchildren that carry, among other things, the marks made by the influence of my life and the wonderful gift of a companion who has walked beside me for more than forty years.

Now more than ever, I feel that I have come home to myself. I am not alienated by my beliefs or a false self. Life is becoming for me what it was destined to be all along. I am thankful for all that is and all that shall be!

20. Hope Beyond

"I think God wants us to be bearers of his Spirit in ordinary conversations because each of us has something to give the other. Until we are ready to listen, we can't receive."

I am ninety-four years old and in pretty good shape for someone who has been around this long. I've gotten so that I don't know anybody as old as I am. Because of my age and because I have been asked to talk about my spiritual journey leading to my thoughts about life beyond, I would like to tell you my story which capsules my journey toward God.

I grew up in a Christian family; thinking of God was as natural as breathing to me. It never occurred to me not to believe in God, but to know the reality of God's presence outside and within me has taken many years. By nature I am a questioner; I have always liked to question ministers to find out what they can tell me about God. I cannot give you an exact date when God became near to me; I didn't have any sudden revelation that turned me from non-believing to believing. My change has been a gradual process of starting and stopping, growing in spurts followed by times of rest. I have questioned a lot, and I have tested the nerves of numerous ministers with all my inquiries about life.

As I have made my journey, there are a number of persons who have had an impact on my life. I will be forever grateful for meeting Frank Laubach, the great preacher, teacher and author of Letters by a Modern Mystic. This man has had a tremendous impact on my life; he was the first person in whom I saw what God really wants to do with each of us. I saw in him a living out of a faith that was so enticing, so real and so vital that I hungered to have that same type of faith; getting to know this man was an indescribable experience. I even had him in my home several times, which precipitated a major point of change.

A Life-Changing Retreat

For one thing, he encouraged me to attend Camp Farthest Out, a weeklong retreat at a campus or center for spiritual renewal. The camps were focused completely on prayer. These gatherings were begun in the 1930s by Dr. Glenn Clark, a Presbyterian college professor with a deep interest in prayer. They have spread across this country and around the world. At Frank Laubach's insistence in 1965 I attended my first camp. After several experiences I was instrumental in starting a Camp Farthest Out in Kentucky. Frank Laubach had promised me that if I would begin a camp, he would come and speak to the group, and he did, not once but twice.

Glenn Clark's books have had a great impact on my life. I met him once and he was fine, just a little roly-poly man, but he didn't have the same qualities that I saw in Frank Laubach. Doubtless, it was my lack of seeing rather than his lack of being. Reading his books had a greater impact upon me than the person himself, though I did not spend much time with him personally. Now Frank Laubach was different; he stands out as one of a kind. But I have read quite widely. I have recently picked up and am re-reading one of Henri Nouwen's books. Nouwen through his writings has made a deep impression on me. Also, Evelyn Underhill has informed me about Christian mysticism. I could go over the many books that I have on my shelves and point out what the different authors have taught me.

The camps have had a terrific impact on people's lives. They always seemed to draw people who were hungry, and spiritual hunger is such a blessing. Until people are hungry, they will not eat. God gives us rich food through people, through circumstances, through books and in all sorts of ways. One of the drawing cards of Camps Farthest Out is the hunger people bring with them. At the camps people from different backgrounds and different denominations attend. I think God wants us to be bearers of his Spirit in ordinary conversations because each of us has something to give the other. Until we are ready to listen, we can't receive.

Frank Laubach had told me to attend one of the camps because the emphasis was always on the spiritual life, the prayer life. I went with a great hunger for deeper prayer in my life. I didn't know about prayer beyond saying, "Now I lay me down to sleep." But to really believe that God through his Spirit comes within us and wills to speak to us and through us is an amazing experience. I have been able to share with people through many situations, but especially in camps. I figure that I have spoken in thirty-five states and almost every continent. I would never have thought this would happen! It is amazing how God wishes to use an empty vessel. It tickles me that God will use a lay person who knows little about theology to speak love to God's people.

I was so ignorant of how God really works. The fact that God is still at work as a healer and a guide to our daily life came as a shock to me. Of course I have received one or two healings, but in our particular church we didn't talk about healing. We thought that was exclusively the business of denominations other than ours. We were a little too intellectual or sophisticated or know-it-all to talk about those supernatural acts of God. So it came as a surprise to me that God was still able to work in ordinary people, to speak through me. I say this without any pride. When God is using you, speaking through you, it gives such joy.

I have been used as an instrument of healing, but it is to God's glory. I know the power of the laying on of hands, though it was something new to me and never was done in my church. Christianity was purely an intellectual acceptance in the church of my birth, and I'm grateful for my church because I've sat under highly intelligent ministers all my life. Living a dynamic faith or putting your hands on somebody would have surprised me to death, and everyone in my church probably would have fainted in the face of such behavior. I belonged to the Disciples of Christ, and we were very smart, just sort of prideful maybe.

I do remember during one of the camps that I had a very strong urge within me to go out of the house and walk barefoot over the grass and touch a tree because I was experiencing such a sense of God's presence, a sense of holiness, a sense of other worldliness that I needed to touch the grass, the earth or a tree that I could identify as real. That may sound crazy, but I do remember it because I was thinking about experiences of God – not a revelation but a realization of God within me. I recall a time of being lifted up in a way that felt as if I were walking like the people who walked through the Red Sea. Something was opening, and I was being led or being called to God. I wish I had a great story to tell about a marvelous revelation, but I do not. What I do have is bits and pieces of truly experiencing the presence of God, like an out of body experience. I seem to have been sensitive to this sort of divine presence, more so than many people. My experience came without my having been taught or having gone to a church where God's living presence was emphasized.

The church that I now attend does have a service of laying on of hands. When this Presbyterian church installed deacons and elders, they did let other ordained people come and kneel down and lay their hands on those being ordained. I remember going to the Holy Land with a couple of Presbyterian ministers. On this tour there was a great sense of God as one of them laid his hands on my head. It was new to him, but I asked him to lay hands on me and there was a great opening as if God was really wanting to touch me.

I think very definitely that my daughter is a miracle. At four and a half months of my pregnancy, I had lost all the fluid that a woman usually loses at the time of birth. The doctor put me to bed and said that I would lose her. I remained in the home with my sister who lived Hopkinsville, Kentucky, which was my home until moving to Atlanta. I went by ambulance and was in bed for four months prior to my daughter's birth because the doctor advised me that my carrying her was a touch and go effort. That was a great time for prayer and time for thinking, and I began to what we now call meditate. I didn't know what meditating was! Still not too good at it!

My Meditation

Meditation is just thinking in the presence of God. For my set time of prayer I use a book from The Upper Room, *A Guide to Prayer for Ministers and Other Servants*. This book of selected readings from the great spiritual leaders of the church has been very helpful for me to begin my quiet time. I read the scripture and then I spend time quieting myself before the Lord and allowing him to think through me when I am open. Usually I write in my quiet time. I always go to my prayer room with pen and paper, and I write down my thoughts. I haven't been engaged lately because I've been painting, and that is a spiritual experience for me at ninety-four. Somebody sent me a box of twenty-four colors that look like crayons, but you put water on the brush and brush the color on a pad. Some of my pictures are fairly good.

For so many years, I thought prayer consisted of just saying words. I recall listening to people stand up in the church and pray each week.

163

They told God exactly what to do, and I had a feeling that was not prayer. God did not need their instruction. So for me prayer is recognizing that God is present, recognizing that God loves me, recognizing God really wants to use a person like me to speak or to love or to simply be the channel of divine love. In my quiet prayer I sometimes have strong feelings, but I don't trust feelings. Feelings are too on again-off again. God promised to be with me, and I assume he's truthful. I've found it so.

I wish that all of us could just realize the creativity that so often lies dormant within us; maybe it is just waiting to be tapped.

The Dark Night

I have certainly experienced darkness; for example, when my first child died. I carried him full term and was in hard labor for three days, nearly dying myself. I know that is not what is typically called "a dark night of the soul," but it was just as dark.

I have learned that there is nothing out of which God can't bring good because nothing is sadder than to have a child die. I know that I have been much more appreciative of my daughter all of her life; God has graced me back giving her such a good disposition and so much love for people. She genuinely loves all kinds of people. I stand in amazement and wonder, "How in the world do you love that person?" When I observe her loving, it seems quite natural for her. It's not an imitation, and it is not an expression that she must work at. I am so extremely thankful for her. She has a daughter and a son, and the daughter now has a baby, making me a great-grandmother. A few days ago we made a picture of four generations. That made me stop and think how really blessed I have been that God has allowed me to live this long.

I think people need pain. Not that you would wish it on them, but I think that you can't really appreciate life unless you are faced with death. You really can't appreciate a sunny day unless you've experienced night. I think God has done a good job at balancing things. Every once in a while I think "God, you must be so smart."

Facing Death

At this point in my life, death doesn't matter; it doesn't make any difference if I am here or there. Should I die today, I would miss a lot of things here, but I have a sneaking suspicion that when we are there, we will know what's going on here. Now whether we can participate in life on earth, I'm not sure. But I do think we will know what's going on here. It's a nice, comfortable feeling, and it's so good that I yearn for everybody to at least know what it's like to have a sense of the divine presence.

Being nearer death doesn't concern me. It's not that I don't want to be with my family here, but I think I'll be with them there eventually, and I'll be with all of my family that have died and gone ahead.

I haven't given any thought to how I would like to be remembered. I really never thought about it. I know my immediate family and a few others that I have met will consider my life. Though I have met lots of people, I don't know whether I left a mark on them that will cause them to remember me.

If people do remember me, I would want them to think of me as I really am. It matters not whether they think I was very spiritual or not; I am beyond that. That holds no importance for me anymore. Honestly, it is not important to me whether they remember me after I'm gone. To be remembered would be nice, I guess, but I'm just grateful for everything that has happened in my life, especially the pain.

What Is Heaven?

I don't think of heaven as a place, yet it is a place. It's one of those things that is not this, but yet it is. Perhaps we'll be aware or maybe our awareness will increase. What we have neglected to see in color and beauty and awe might somehow shine more brightly and questions will emerge. . ."Why didn't I see better? Why didn't I hear better? Why didn't I feel my life more?" I think that heaven is life at the fullest. At times I ask myself, is it real or not, but I believe with all my heart that it is real. I believe that the essence of me and the essence of God in me will grow forever and ever.

I don't go in too much for hell. Not that I don't think people suffer. I think we have to suffer for what we do. I think there's a result, but I don't think God is going to say, "Well, you've done this or that and that was too much." I just don't believe that God will exclude people from his presence forever. When you get older, you become needier and softer, and perhaps that is what is happening to me.

Life seems sort of hazy, and we go through our days somewhat hazy; our vision is not sharp. All of us have certain things that we regret, but God forgives us and that makes life all right again. He makes all things right! He makes all things good, and I think that he wants all of us to enjoy what he has made. I think we will learn to enjoy God and be grateful for all the gifts given to us.

I believe that it takes a longer time for some of us to get it right. I don't think it's just an instant, sudden transformation from here to there. It seems to me that there will be a process of growth even after death. We will be transformed and have a deeper appreciation for that other dimension. It's like another dimension of life, an eye-opener that you don't see too well at first. I think there will be change in heaven. I definitely believe in growth in our future life; it will not be a static state, good or bad. And I think that from heaven we will affect things here on earth. If you are interested in things on earth, I think that in heaven God will impart to us something that we are able to hand down. I don't know what you would call that, but it is an expectation that I hold.

I once asked a minister if people in heaven look down and see us as we are today. He said, "How could they be happy because we are making such a mess of things." I was just about twelve years old when I asked that question, and the minister didn't attempt to answer it in a way I could understand. Today I think that heaven is much closer than we think. Why, I think heaven is right here in this room. I think that our awareness opens a way for God to do something that he doesn't do otherwise. I think that shaking people up and making them aware is probably the greatest gift that any of us can give another.

What Is Important Now?

I have come to believe that there is nothing more important than our being quiet before God and learning to be centered in God. We need to do away with extraneous and superfluous things. We also must do away with the prideful attitudes we hold, do away with everything that feeds our egos. We need most to place ourselves before God daily. I think of this as lying in the sun. I used to just love to lie in the sun in my swimming suit, just lie there and feel the warmth of the sun on my body and allow the sun to gradually change the color of my skin. In the presence of God, to be fully there, be present, and not be thinking of other things like duties or past sins or about people you don't like, not thinking of anything, but simply being there allowing yourself to be transformed by God.

21. A View from Beyond: A Vision of Heaven

Sometimes it's very appropriate
to picture ourselves
as naturally living
our final day of life,
to sincerely experience it quite fully
and to venture into
a deeper, quieter yielding
leading to a vaster Yes.

Sometimes this is
what one needs—
to revere
the wavy green grass
carpeting an infinitely blue sky
and one's highest efforts,
and the next simple thing to do,
and, most especially,
those ones receiving
our total open heart
and our unabashed
commitment to love--
to see it all
for the very last time,
knowing that the real race
has been run
and the grander victory
has been won.

And to revere,
with awe,
all we hoped to be,
and
are being,
is to know it
as already given.

Even our weary and battered heart,
threadbare from too much trying,
too much giving,
too much fragility.

And, in the blink of the eye,
everything changes
and it all becomes
one gentle Opus
of Love's majestic intentions.

So let us go now,
relax in our reserved seat
in the reflective Bleachers
of Afterlife
and
take our places
and look back through time and space
at everything we experience today.

Observe without a single care
an imperfectly perfect life well lived;
embrace every undesirable feature,
every moment of fear and constriction,
every numbed out cell in our body,
every unfulfilled hope and dream.

We, I venture to say,
shall weep without ceasing
with overwhelming joy
and gratitude
flowing from every salty tear
and every nanosecond of energy
as our eyes of truth
see the Great Mercy
of things
as they are.

In a single flash
we come
to the climactic realization
and overwhelming enlightenment
that everything we fully knew
before we were born
and everything we totally forgot
at our birth
now culminates,
reunites and claims
that greatest trophy—
true conscious wisdom
earned
through genuinely refined
and sacrificial
suffering.

Remember what the Man said:
"There is no greater love than this,
that a person lay down one's life
for the other."

So, we sit calmly
and equitably
in our
respective
psychic
death lodges.

We invite everyone
and anything we ever
cherished
and wished to possess for our own;
we let them all come
and receive and give
final blessings
as we prepare
body and soul
to inherit the Great Mercy.

This, by the way,
is not merely poetic exercise;
it is not merely active imagination.
It is the stuff
from which
mud and stars,
life and death
and
life forever
are born.

Hal Edwards

22. A Physician/Pastor Turns Toward Death and Life

*"Living with death, living 'in hospice' means living,
intentionally, purposefully, hopefully."*

My call, I thought, was to be a missionary physician, not a hospice physician. When I graduated unexpectedly early from college (my last required course having been rescheduled from spring to fall), I enrolled in Columbia Theological Seminary as a "special student," dabbling in courses across the curriculum, choosing those topics I thought might make me a better doctor. At that time, many of the pastoral courses in which I was interested were restricted to Master of Divinity candidates; undeterred, I enrolled in the Master of Divinity Program.

I had not planned on marriage. My father (who, himself, had a dual career as an attorney and an airline pilot) had told me all my life that there were many things I would have to give up in order to study medicine, and marriage was one of those necessary sacrifices. I was stunned and terrified when I first saw Bill sitting across the room at an after-worship social, because I knew immediately that he and I would be married. We had not yet even met, and there was no "love at first sight"; just the absolute certainty that we would commit our lives to one another. Later that evening, I learned that he had grown up in the Congo, the son and grandson of missionaries, and had returned there after college to teach mathematics at a high school at Katubue. I dated him reluctantly, mostly because an Egyptian seminary classmate kept setting me up with him. I told him "No," quite firmly, each of the three times he asked me to marry him, even though I had begun to love him deeply.

The following fall, on the first day of medical school, I asked the Dean how to register for New Testament Greek. Her response was a stern lecture, delivered in full view and hearing of my classmates, people who would be my colleagues for the rest of my medical career. "Aren't you committed to becoming a physician?" she asked.

"This will take everything you have, and if you are not willing to focus on this goal, it is not too late to call up someone on the waiting list." I determined then that it was probably unwise to mention Hebrew and Church History, for which I was registered at the seminary.

In contrast to the response of the medical school administration, the seminary community (students, faculty and administration) couldn't have been more supportive. Course sections were scheduled when I could come, class notes were supplied, and the faculty occasionally invented courses I needed. Eventually several of my medical school professors, who were also elders on various church and presbytery committees, became aware of what I was doing and lent their support. My medical school classmates gave me a variety of nicknames, and teased me about "hatching, matching and dispatching" my patients, but came to talk with me, like Nicodemuses in the night, when their patients died or their marriages were troubled.

Bill and I were wed on Saint Patrick's Day of my first year of medical school. It was 1973, and contract marriages were all the rage. Many of our friends, and all sorts of handbooks on marriage, suggested that marriages were more likely to be successful if partners figured out ahead of time how long they planned to be together, and who was going to do which chores. We debated for weeks about what to promise one another, until finally I made my best offer: fifty years, and then he would get twenty-four hours to look around and see if he could do better. "I'll take it," he immediately said with a big grin.

I graduated from seminary in 1982, still not anticipating ordination, still not under the care of presbytery. During that summer, however, I received three completely unsought calls to ministries which required ordination. Finally, I figured out that perhaps God was trying to tell me something, and began the candidacy process. A year later, I accepted the call to be a chaplain in the hospice of Grady, Atlanta's metropolitan hospital, and was ordained to the ministry of Word and Sacrament. Dr. Mel Moore, the medical director of the hospice and an oncologist, immediately sent me to Connecticut Hospice to take their physician training. What I remember most vividly about that program, and about that period of my medical career, was the friendship of much older female physicians, women who had "left" medicine for many years to rear their children and honor their marriages, but who returned to medical careers in their sixties, to care for people who were critically underserved: the mentally ill, the Appalachian poor, and the dying. I had some personal heroines.

That was the most formative period of my life. I became a physician with the support of colleagues and the wisdom of my department chair (himself an elder in a local congregation). I became a pastor in a ministry supervised by a gifted hospice director, who was also a hospital chaplain. I became a wife, nurtured and supported by a loving congregation of couples who could model those roles well. I became a mother with a company of other mothers and a wonderful pediatrician, whom I had chosen because he was the person I wanted to see across my sons' beds when they had leukemia or major trauma. Instead, I found I really needed him when the boys had some rash or their teachers called me (again!) about their "exuberant" behavior.

Being a hospice chaplain confirmed what I had realized shortly before my ordination: my call was to pastoral ministry, and medicine was to be my entry way into the lives of patients, families and communities. People who were dealing with physical ailments and health-related crises welcomed me into their lives and families, into the private spaces of which they were often unaware, into empty spiritual places. What an extraordinary privilege! That realization spilled over into my clinical practice as well. I began to become comfortable with the fact that I am a "package deal." I cannot dissect myself or compartmentalize myself for one occasion or another. I care about the physical, psychological and spiritual wellbeing of whole persons, and am called to bring all my skills to that care.

Transition: Finding My Niches

I served as the Grady hospice chaplain for two years and very briefly as the medical director of another hospice. In the following years, I continued practicing Family Medicine in a neighborhood clinic of Grady, mostly on a half-time basis. During the rest of my time, I evaluated developmentally delayed folks for county services, served as a clinic physician in a Teen Obstetrics Clinic, opened the first lactation center in Georgia, cared for imprisoned teenagers and offered health care to the homeless. All of those were opportunities to be welcomed into families, to share in their pain and triumphs. In each one, I worked with people of deep faith, with whom I frequently prayed and studied Scripture, and occasionally officiated at weddings and funerals.

Our sons, who were two and three when I was ordained, were joined by a "surprise" ten years younger than they were. The older boys grew up and left for college, and Bill became the full-time parent of our family while I continued to work. My father developed dementia, and we began "the long goodbye"; after his death, my mother moved to Atlanta to live near us in a retirement center.

One of the most rewarding developments in my life at that time was becoming the very unofficial campus physician at Columbia Seminary. I simply passed around my contact information, introduced myself during orientation, and was available for students, and faculty, who needed healthcare, but couldn't access it. I also served on several denominational task forces, chairing a subcommittee on health missions, drafting the tobacco policy of the Presbyterian Church (USA), interpreting our alcohol policy, and moderating our Health and Serious Mental Illness networks. Again, I was privileged to work with families and people of deep faith and faithfulness to the Church.

I remember great stress and unhappiness during this time as each of the so-fulfilling parts of my life competed with the others. However, I also remember this long period as one that was rich and full of life. Perhaps that is so because, in retrospect, I learned so much to prepare me for what was to follow. So does God heal our memories?

Transition: A Friend Dies

One of the most memorable and formative experiences of this period in my life was the death of Lucy Rose. Lucy was a professor of homiletics at Columbia Theological Seminary, a chair to which she came after I had graduated. I had heard that she had breast cancer, and I prayed for her frequently when I attended chapel, but we didn't meet one another while she was undergoing her initial treatment, or even after her cancer metastasized and she began palliative chemotherapy. Several of our mutual friends began urging me to get in touch with her; those same people urged her to be in touch with me. Both of us resisted the urgings. She told people that she wasn't comfortable calling up a physician she didn't know and asking for free care. I explained to people that I don't just call someone and tell them I am a physician with experience in helping dying people, and "you need me." Besides, I was aware that Lucy already had a close friend from her worshiping community who is a nurse and an extraordinary adviser and coach.

One evening, however, Lucy had such severe pain in her chest that she and her friend simply couldn't get ahead of it, and her friend called me. I remember being deeply touched, and deeply regretting that I had not reached out to Lucy after all, a decision which forced her to come to me when she was very vulnerable and in great pain. There were so many possibilities that chest pain in the setting of metastatic breast cancer might represent, that I couldn't know what was happening without some diagnostic studies, so we went to an Emergency Room, where a chest x-ray was done. The technician brought the film into Lucy's room and put it up on the light box behind Lucy but in view of me. It was devastating, her lungs full of fluid and obvious metastatic disease. There was a long moment of silence between us, and then Lucy asked, "I'm in real trouble now?" I nodded. In my heart I promised God and myself that no one would ever again have to learn of his or her dying from me while I was a stranger, if there were anything I could do to avoid it.

Over the following weeks, I came to deeply love Lucy, her husband and child, and her extended families, both biological and ecclesiastic. They welcomed me as one of them, caring for me as they had been caring for one another all along. Many years later, facing life-threatening illness myself, I re-read Lucy's journal and my own account of her dying. It brought back vivid memories of laughter and tears, prayers and visits of the Spirit, understandings of Scripture and experiences of pastoral ministry. As Lucy began actively dying, her students sang hymns on her porch, as they had done for hours. Inside her room, she listened to tapes of the Psalms and the Gospel of John, created the previous week and overnighted to her as a parting gift from her colleagues in the Academy of Homiletics. Her parents and siblings came and went from her room, caring for her daughter, and alternately giving Lucy and her husband both cherished company and intimate privacy in which to say goodbyes. I waited in her living room with her teaching partner and one of her childhood friends whom I had known for many years, and we talked with deep pain about how we wanted to die as she was doing, in the midst of family, friends, church and Spirit.

It was the first planning I had done for my own death, and years later, that conversation would mark the beginning of my own dying to me.

Transition: Becoming a Widow

Bill and our middle son had become bicycling enthusiasts, and together one summer they had completed BRAG, the annual Bike Ride Across Georgia. The following year, Bill went for a ride while we were vacationing in Montreat, NC, and did a "face plant" after hitting a rock and sailing over his handlebars. He came home under his own steam, but was scraped and sore, and was convinced he had broken a rib.

Over the next several months, the rest of him healed, but the rib kept aching, and he developed musculoskeletal pain he thought was arthritis. Then he began to lose weight, and I began to fear the worst. He made an appointment with a physician who was also a dear friend from among the parents of our youngest son's Scout troop. However, the appointment was on a day during the Presbyterian Church's General Assembly, to which I was taking some youth who were completing their God and Life Award for Scouting and Camp Fire. I called the friend, explained the situation, and asked if he would do a chest x-ray before I left – I didn't want to have to make a U-turn on I-75 if Bill had any serious problem. He said of course, set up the film, and called to let me know that it looked fine and he would call me if he found anything worrisome when he examined Bill.

Two days later, we were settled in a yurt in a state park, and the children were working on the scavenger hunt the other chaperone and I had created for them, when our physician friend left a message for me to call him. Bill almost certainly had advanced prostate cancer; would I be able to get home safely? I was reeling, unable to breathe or think for the fears racing through my mind. Anne, the other chaperone, who was a Presbyterian elder and a widow herself, quietly assumed leadership of the retreat and managed to care for me at the same time. When I got home, Bill and I prayed together, then clung to one another in silence.

We told our sons and Bill's parents, who came home to Atlanta from Virginia where they spent their summers. Annette, Bill's stepmother, is a nurse who had gone to Zaire at the same time Bill had. Our lives began to spin, taking on new shapes on an hourly basis, as Bill's workup was completed and his treatment plan was developed.

Mary Jane, our pastor since she and I had graduated together from seminary, called me faithfully every night of Bill's dying, to talk and to pray with me. I remember telling her in tears one night how much I dreaded the separation, the drifting apart, that I had so often witnessed in couples when I had been a hospice chaplain. I did not want Bill to die before he died; I did not want my sons to lose their father before he left us.

But, leave us he did. The rib pain and "arthritis" he had been feeling were bone metastases, and the ones in his spine were compressing the nerves to his legs. They threatened him with paralysis, and as soon as his bone scan was read, the Radiation Oncologist called us back for emergency radiation treatments. As the metastatic cells die of radiation burns, they swell, making the risk of paralysis even greater, so high dose steroids are given at the same time as the radiation. In his hospital room, we hugged one another in his bed, shielding one another from the literal and figurative dark surrounding us, while understanding nurses quietly offered their care, and smiled their approval of our cramped sleeping arrangement that was keeping us sane. As soon as the immediate danger of paralysis was past, we came home from the hospital, and Bill began physical therapy as an outpatient to regain the muscle strength he had lost in his legs.

However, he became psychotic from the steroids.

One day, Annette called me at work and said Bill seemed short of breath, so over my lunch hour, I dashed home with the clinic oximeter to check his oxygen saturation. It was in the 80s, critically low, and we made arrangements for a trip to the Emergency Room. He had developed viral brain and lung infections because of the immunosuppression of the steroids, and just as the psychosis began to recede, he became encephalopathic. Throughout the summer, he worsened in spite of hormonal treatments, and entered a rehabilitation facility for a month of more intense physical therapy.

Then, as autumn deepened, he slowly came back to us, in physical strength and coordination, but far more importantly, in personality and thinking. Our witty, pun-making, fun-loving, outdoorsman was home. Once again, we could plan and dream and hope, pray together, love our sons and one another. Our life together righted itself, and became unexpectedly and unexplainably rich. The last months of our marriage were the best months of our marriage.

When Bill began to decline again after the Christmas holidays, we sat down with each of our sons and asked them if there were any unfinished things they wanted to do with Bill, while he felt well enough to do them. Both our older sons said they "were good" with their dad, that they had had over twenty full years together, and that they wanted their younger brother to have all the time that could be squeezed out to create the kind of memories they cherished. That son, John, said that he wanted to finish his Eagle project with his dad; so, as a family, and as a community of friends and neighbors, we began a race against time.

On the morning of John's Board of Review, I could not awaken Bill, and his breathing had become ragged. He was "in transition," a technical term for us in hospice, indicating that he was "actively dying," and his death was imminent. The Board of Review for Eagle was relocated from the familiarity of our Scout Hut, to our next door neighbor's front porch. While the rest of the family began our vigil with Bill, John "stood" his review. He came running home across our front yard, tears streaming down his face, into the bedroom where we were waiting, saying, "Dad, Dad, I did it. I made Eagle." I thought Bill was comatose, but he reached out with the hand in which I had placed John's Eagle medal, and gave it to John. As a family, and as a community, we had won the race; death would not deny us that last gift.

The remainder of the day was luxurious, as time seemed to stand still. Together, we reminisced about favorite vacations, laughed about one another's eccentricities, made puns that occasionally prompted the trace of a smile on Bill's lips. We felt bathed in prayer, and held close by Love, and healed. About 2:30 the next morning, Bill's breathing became very shallow. John slipped his arm under Bill's shoulders, cradling him, as our middle son, James, began to sing "Swing Low, Sweet Chariot." It was a bedtime song Bill sang to them while playing his guitar, a lullaby in our family. As the four of us sang him Home, Bill slowly stopped breathing. It was Holy Saturday of 2003.

Transition: Facing My Own Death

One afternoon in the spring of 2014 I talked with my sister, Michele. She used to weigh more than I did, but she had started and stuck to a diet, and was down to a beautiful, healthy size six. I wanted that, too. I had lost about forty pounds several years earlier, and then plateaued.

I wanted so badly to get off of "stuck" and begin losing again, so I had gone on her diet, and really stayed with it.

And lost nothing. Not one measly ounce.

So that afternoon, I had called her, pleading for advice. "Don't worry about not losing weight," she had said. "Don't even get on the scales. Think in terms of dress size. Go buy yourself something a little snug, and see how quickly you can get into it comfortably."

That evening, I lay on the floor, poking my belly, trying to see if I felt any skinnier.

What I felt was a mass in my pelvis. Firm. Huge. A lump with lumps.

The next morning I made an appointment with the friend who had delivered all my sons. The earliest one I could get was almost two weeks away.

Night after night, I prodded and poked, trying to tell if it were getting bigger, if it were mobile, if I could tell what organ it was from. I couldn't think of anything "safe" it could be. Uterine fibroids wouldn't be so bad, but fibroids take estrogen to grow, and I hadn't produced any of that for a long time. I searched the Internet, and what I read only confirmed my worst fears. Ovarian cancer is the most common malignant tumor in women my age, and isn't usually discovered until it is advanced, frequently far metastasized from the ovary in which it began, creeping on to neighboring structures, out of the pelvis, peppering the omentum, invading other organs. The life expectancy of a woman with ovarian cancer is usually measured in months.

The day my friend was to check me finally arrived. His nurse asked me the introductory questions about when I had had my last Pap smear and did I practice self-breast exams. When Asher entered the exam room, we bantered a minute about old times, former colleagues, our children, and then he asked me what had brought me in. I answered that I felt a mass in my pelvis, and his head and his nurse's popped up. No one spoke as he did the examination; no one had to say what all of us were thinking.

Following an examination, the next step is a pelvic ultrasound, but his ultrasonographer had been in a motor vehicle crash earlier in the week and wasn't back in the office yet. I made an appointment for the following Friday.

Her bedside manner was lovely. She moved the transducer gently but firmly, apologizing for any discomfort she caused me (though there was no discomfort to the study), conversing as she measured and mapped. When she was finished, she invited me to get dressed while she showed the images to Asher.

He walked into the room and sat down in a chair beside me. "Well," he began, "you do have fibroids."

"Asher," I responded, "is that all I have?"

"No," he answered, shaking his head, his eyes tearing. "No, Marilyn, I am so sorry. It looks like an ovarian mass, and it's twelve centimeters big." He handed me the report, already typed and printed. Twelve centimeters, as big across as a CD – how had I missed that? How long had it been there? I hadn't asked the questions aloud, but my friend guessed what I was thinking. "I'm going to tell you what you already know," he said. "You didn't do anything to get this, and it didn't get this big because you missed some Pap smears. Ovarian tumors just grow quickly. Don't beat yourself up."

I scanned the report for other data. I would read it over and over the next few days, until I had it nearly memorized. The most important thing in it, even more than the size, was the fact that the tumor had both solid and cystic components, and the cystic portions contained walls of tissue, dividing the cysts into smaller pockets of fluid – heterogeneous tissue, thick septa, a "prominent" lymph node – all characteristics of malignancy.

Back at home, I called our three sons and asked for an emergency family meeting, to be held on Sunday afternoon at James and Rachel's home. Around their dining table with our twin granddaughters playing in the nearby rooms, I told the guys as honestly and fully as I could what probably lay ahead. We cried together, then sat in silence together. On the way to my mother's apartment, I called my in-laws in Virginia; after I told my mother, I called my sister. Finally, I called my dear friend and seminary classmate, who had been our pastor when Bill was dying.

I wanted to tell my colleagues in ministry myself, rather than have them read about me in a newsletter. There was no way to tell everyone at once, but there was a meeting of pastors in my area that week, and I called the convener of that meeting to let him know what was going on and what I wanted to say. When the meeting began, he gave me the floor, and I told the group that I probably had ovarian cancer. Joe suggested that they pray for me before going on with the meeting, and the woman sitting next to me stood and put her hands on my head and shoulder. The rest of the group followed her lead, and this gathering of the Teaching Elders prayed for me in the oh-so-Biblical tradition. I remember thinking how protected I felt, surrounded by their fervor and love. That memory sustained me not only through the following weeks, but also through all the health crises I could not imagine in that moment.

Asher had referred me to the medical complex where I had taught, as I requested, and I was seen the following Monday by a female surgeon. She examined me, as Asher had done, and ordered an MRI. She also scheduled me for an evaluation by an internist whom I didn't know, and didn't want to see; I knew I needed a primary care physician who would really take care of all of me, not do a "quickie" evaluation of the murmur I had had since at least medical school. Since this didn't feel like a time to share my life with other strangers, I canceled the appointment which had been made for me, and called two health care providers for appointments: a friend I had been intending to ask to be my primary care provider, and my mother's cardiac nurse practitioner. Both of them understood the urgency of getting these preparatory examinations and surgical clearances, and worked me into their schedules.

Kristen, the cardiac nurse practitioner, asked if I could come to her office that morning and saw me fifteen minutes after I called. She thought the murmur might be coming from my aortic valve and suggested a stress test to evaluate it. That was planned for the following Monday. I wasn't very worried about the murmur because I had had it so long, and because it had been heard by so many medical classmates and colleagues. I actually anticipated the study with curiosity rather than anxiety. And the study was fascinating. "My" team consisted of a nurse, an ultrasonographer and a cardiology fellow, who clearly understood what the diagnosis of an ovarian mass signified and why I was so eager to get the study completed so I could get on to surgery. The ultrasonographer positioned her screen so I could see it while lying on my side on a gurney. The nurse gave me the medication which causes the heart to race. I could feel it pounding, faster and harder, as the medicine increased, but every step of the process had been thoroughly explained beforehand, and as each step approached, the nurse reminded me what to expect next. I knew I was being continuously monitored. My heart was the least of my worries at that moment, and the stress test was something of an intellectual diversion.

When it was completed, the fellow assured me that my aortic valve was never going to be a problem – "a little calcium in the leaflet," he said, and turned to the ultrasonographer to ask, "Do you see anything else that needs pursuing?"

"Well," she answered gently, "what do you think of that lesion in her left anterior descending artery?"

Silence fell like a great weight in the room. The fellow peered at the films; I held my breath. The attending was called; I was grilled about any chest pain I had felt. There had never been pain; I felt fine; I just wanted to get rid of this tumor.

But I was not fine. The following day, I underwent a cardiac catheterization, which confirmed what they and I feared – I had significant coronary atherosclerotic heart disease. A small stent was placed in the worst of the stenotic arteries, and I began a month of blood thinners before I could go to surgery. Two days later, I had a gastrointestinal bleed, necessitating another hospitalization and emergency colonoscopy, which uncovered a small polyp, but there was nothing that could be done about that while my heart healed and the anticoagulants continued.

I refused sedation for the endoscopy, as I had done for the cardiac catheterizations and stenting. I did not know that decision would trigger a consultation with an anesthesiologist, who asked, "Dr. Washburn, what are your fears about anesthesia? Can we talk about that?" I explained that I am not a heroine about pain, but I did dread the nausea and vomiting that I have had every time I have had narcotics. That fear had led me to refuse anesthesia and pain relief in the past, even after a Cesarean birth. "Then let's come up with a plan for your pelvic surgery," she responded, and in just a few memorable minutes she asked questions, made suggestions, and helped me draft an anesthesia plan for the anesthesiologists who would care for me during surgery. That young woman treated me with dignity and respect and compassion, really listened to my fears, and addressed them with practical advice. I will bless her name and her work for the remainder of my life.

The month crept past. I interviewed two more surgeons, choosing an older woman, Stephanie, with whom I felt instantly comfortable and who wanted to try to do my procedure robotically. I completed three weeks of cardiac rehabilitation, a wonderful experience of community and encouragement. I read all I could find about ovarian cancer, forced myself to memorize the fairly grim statistics, and imagined the details of various treatment options. I did not feel like I had time for the luxury of denial. An attorney-neighbor helped me set up a trust fund and rewrite my will, and I went to a funeral home, where an extremely compassionate funeral director helped me make the choices necessary to spare my sons that burden. A cousin sent me a "chemo quilt" featuring a shepherd and sheep, on which she embroidered the 23rd Psalm, and I wrapped myself in its warmth to meditate and pray. Friends and family, and especially colleagues in ministry, called to let me know they were praying for me. Fellow Scouters set up a campership fund in my honor, and imagining youngsters learning life skills in the outdoors gave me great joy. My closest friend from childhood, with whom I had lost contact, called to share memories and tears.

A seminary friend, who was also an RN, had trained in hypnosis and offered to give me some instruction. Initially reluctant, I did an Internet search and couldn't think of any way that would interfere with cardiac rehabilitation or surgery. I accepted her invitation, renewing an old and cherished friendship, and learning a pain control technique that I hoped would minimize my post-operative recovery time. She wrote a script for self-hypnosis prior to the surgery, and together we amended it to be based on the 139th Psalm. I loved the imagery of God's Spirit searching me as I knew the light of the surgeon's robot would do, and the affirmation that my body is good, even it were invaded by cancer. I practiced the breathing and script daily, and the practice reminded me of the imaging and relaxation Bill and I had done in childbirth classes so many years before. I liked that image, too, preparing to birth new life with Bill partnering with me in that memory.

Meanwhile, I rapidly lost weight, and the tumor became easier to feel; I couldn't tell if that were true because I was shrinking so quickly or because it was growing. One night, I awakened with a rapid heart rate and profuse sweating, and suspected I was having a heart attack. I remember wondering if my prayer for a quick death, rather than protracted dying from cancer, was being answered, but I never felt any chest pain and eventually fell back asleep. Later, after surgery, I would learn that the tumor had ruptured and hemorrhaged.

I had told my in-laws that they needn't come back from Virginia for the surgery, but they insisted, and I realized how deeply comforting it was to have family to wait with our sons, and with whom to pray. They reserved rooms in a nearby motel, where we spent the night prior to my operation, and our sons joined us for dinner. Afterward, as we walked back to the motel, I asked them for their blessings. They prayed with me, and I slept soundly.

When we arrived to check in the following morning, I was moved to tears to find that my "team" had already arrived. This was a complete surprise, since I had suspected our sons wouldn't handle the wait very well, and I had asked them not to come. Instead, our middle son sent his wife, and my oldest son's wife, whose baby was only a few weeks old, sent her mother! My pastor, too, was there, and the pastor of the congregation I had begun attending came as well. Mary Jane insisted that everyone join me in the pre-op area for Communion, and, while she led the family back to the waiting area, Tom followed my gurney to the very door of the operating room.

The anesthesiologist and anesthetist asked again if I were sure I didn't want sedation or narcotic analgesics, shrugged their shoulders when I again declined those medications, and the anesthetist said, "Then, let's get this nap started." I went to sleep praying the 139th Psalm.

I gently became aware of my surroundings in the PACU, the post-anesthesia care unit, as my gurney was juggled into a curtained niche, and there was busy-ness all around me. I didn't feel anything in my abdomen, and, puzzled, I moved my hand to the place I thought the dressing would be.

There was no dressing.

There was no port for intraperitoneal chemotherapy.

There was no pain.

For an instant, the thought occurred to me that perhaps Stephanie had had to abort the surgery altogether. I peeked under the blanket at my abdomen – there were five short incisions, clean and dry, and crusty with surgical glue.

I palpated my abdomen, tentatively at first and then with growing pressure. The emptiness inside me was a delicious feeling. Finally, the tumor was gone, and Stephanie had done it all laparoscopically. I remember smiling, joyful that "the thing" was out of me. I realized I was in the PACU because of all the other patients being rolled in and out around me, understanding immediately that I had not had a "cardiac event," else I would be surrounded by the beeping machines of an ICU instead of the well-organized chaos that filled this room. I knew that whatever Stephanie and the pathologists had found, and whatever lay ahead in terms of treatment, that cardiac stability and the robotically assisted laparoscopy would move me to the next steps in far less recovery time. I waited for her to come explain what she had found, what she had done, and what my immediate future held.

Without my glasses, I could not see her when she arrived, but I recognized Stephanie's voice when she spoke to me, and all the other noises dropped to the background.

"It was benign," she said. "I did the abdominal washings, but there was no need to finish the staging."

My disbelief was overwhelming. After all that had gone wrong in the previous eight weeks, could the most important thing really have gone right? Not sure I could speak coherently yet, I put all my effort into the words: "Are they sure?" Stephanie chuckled quietly. (Oh, how I love that chuckle!) "Yes," she said, "they are sure."

There would be time, later, for the details. Right then, needing to be alone with my thoughts and prayers, I curled into the warm blankets spread over me, beginning to store memories and insights as they raced through my awakening mind. In that moment I realized I had parted paths with Bill. I felt as though I had abandoned him, taking the path of life instead of death, as if I had somehow really chosen. I missed him more than ever, wanted to share this joy with him more than anyone else, wanted him to be my partner in this new life I was entering. I wept, not bitterly or violently, but quietly with sorrow for him, for all he had missed: the weddings, John's graduation and extraordinary Scouting career, the granddaughters, the trips. I wept for a marriage, now completed. I wept for joy at the prospect of a whole new life which lay ahead of me. I wept with gratitude that my children were spared the anguish of another parental loss, and that our grandchildren would know at least one of us. I wept for the future he could not share with me.

Stephanie visited my family in the waiting area as I had asked her to do, reassuring them that the tumor was a benign cyst, and that she had been able to remove it without an abdominal incision. I had left a list of people to notify – my mother-in-law took the phone calls, and my daughter-in-law, the e-mails. (My brother, a leukemia survivor, sailing in the Pacific Ocean somewhere, sent word that he was delighted to know he would have a "cyster" for a long time to come.)

I was in the PACU for about three hours, while the staff searched for a bed for me. Awake, fully aware, excited to be contemplating an indefinite future, I felt no anxiety and no impatience. I knew my family had been told the good news, and were celebrating as they awaited reunion with me; I wanted for nothing; I felt luxuriously pampered – was I warm, was I comfortable, did I have pain, was there anything the nurses could get for me? I could have rested content forever in the relief and freedom and newness I felt.

An "overflow bed" was found for me in the Women's Center. I hadn't given any thought to where I would recover and spend the first night, but somehow it appealed to me, and comforted me, that I was in a Women's Center, being cared for among other women, by women. I had tasted something of an experience that only women have. By this point, I was thirty pounds slimmer than at the beginning of the summer, the invasion of my feminine anatomy had ended, and the organs I had always associated with the joy of giving birth could never betray me. I felt silly for having the feelings, but I felt beautiful, inside and out, and I was grateful that I didn't have to even think about how incongruent the feeling was with the image in the mirror.

The gurney was rolled beside my bed, and the bed was raised to meet it. I braced for serious pain as I started to slide across the gap from gurney to bed. I lifted my legs gingerly one after another – no pain. I lifted my trunk and shifted my weight to the bed – no pain. Elated, I realized there was going to be no pain, no pain at all in this recovery. I wiggled with vigor to the bed, and as the gurney was rolled out of the room, dangled my feet off the side.

"I want to walk," I implored the nurse immediately. "Could I please just try standing up and walking, maybe just to the chair and back?"

"Of course," she smiled brightly, without hesitation or delay. I had expected some pushback, some reluctance to let me up and about so quickly. After all, I had just had a hysterectomy, tumor excision and salpingo-oophorectomy. When I trained in gynecology, that bought you at least a day of enforced bedrest. "Let's tackle the hallway," she encouraged. And so, as my family exited the elevator to see me for the first time after surgery, I met and hugged them in the hallway while their cellphone cameras recorded the moment.

We walked back to my room together, I pushing my IV pole alongside me. Family and friends came and went through the afternoon, and the returning calls, texts and e-mails were relayed to me in "real time." I never felt tired, irritable or uncomfortable, but I wanted to know everything about the two hours of my life I had missed. What did they talk about while they were waiting? What, exactly, had Stephanie said to them? How had they reacted? What had my friends and extended family said when they heard the news? In a strange way I felt cheated that I couldn't be at my own life celebration. The following morning I went home, and a few days later, Stephanie called me. She identified herself, but skipped all the perfunctory greetings: "The final pathology shows your tumor was a benign struma ovarii," she said.

"Then, it's really over?" I asked, still incredulous that the epidemiology and the radiology had been so misleading.

"Yes," she answered, and I could hear the grin in her voice. "It is finally over."

Transition: Becoming a Full-Time Hospice Physician

A few weeks after the surgery, I went to lunch with the retired pastor who organized the clergy cluster meetings in our presbytery. I told him that I realized my current job was not a healthy one for me. I was reviewing cases to be sure that they were appropriate for Medicare reimbursement, working in my pajamas from my back bedroom. The work was intellectually challenging, but completely sedentary and high pressure.

"What do you want to do?" he asked. "Oh, Joe," I answered. "I want to be doing whatever it is God is calling me to do – I just can't figure that out."

"Let's try a different tack," he suggested. "What have you liked doing?" That answer didn't require any deliberation. "I loved patient care, but I won't be practicing long enough to rebuild that. I loved hospice, and I loved teaching." "Got it," he said, and we finished lunch. A week later a hospice chaplain contacted me and asked if I wanted to meet after the next presbytery meeting. When we did, she said, "We don't have any chaplaincy positions open in our hospice right now, but we are recruiting physicians. Would you consider that?" "All of what you see is what you get," I replied.

I applied for the position, had an interview with the General Manager and the Medical Director, and began work in a per diem capacity, hoping that in six months to a year they would like me and I would like them, and I could move to full time. Six weeks later, the General Manager called me into her office and offered me a full-time position, which I accepted.

Occasionally, friends or colleagues gently tease me about having specialized in a field in which all my patients die, suggesting that there is no more urgency, no more pressure, nothing I can do wrong in that setting. I know differently, because when time to create memories and heal relationships is short, my care must be the most patient and sensitive I have ever given. If my patients and their families are to have no regrets, are to remember their lives together with thanksgiving and joy, are to die with dignity in spite of all the indignities of their disease, everyone on the hospice team must offer exquisitely competent and tender care.

My first patient in a full-time capacity was Steve Hayner, the president of Columbia Seminary from which I had graduated, whom I knew about but had not met. He and his wife, Sharol, and their daughter, Emilie, had been sharing their journey in publicly accessible blogs since he was diagnosed with pancreatic cancer nine months earlier. At my first visit, he met me at the door – not a typical experience among hospice families! We were a bit formal, he and his wife and I, sitting in their living room, asking one another questions that were still somewhat mechanical and even superficial, questions about symptom control and how we could contact one another.

Later that week, referring to all the conversations they had had with our entire hospice team, Sharol wrote:

....beginning the journey with hospice brings amazing relief. Someone else now takes responsibility for Steve's meds. Someone with training in end-of-life issues is watching over his care. When we arrived home after making the decision to enroll in hospice, Steve confessed that he felt strangely encouraged. I, too, was encouraged. We feel deep peace over this decision even though the reality of Steve's death stares us in the face.

The following weeks were full of transitions for them, as their lives were shifted over and over again by Steve's illness. One of the first transitions was from their oncology team to their hospice team. They and their hospice nurse developed a friendship marked simultaneously by lighthearted cheer and serious attention to Steve's worsening symptoms. They and their hospice chaplain had worshipped together in a local congregation for a long while, and Steve had served as an important mentor to that younger pastor. Now, their roles changed, as the chaplain offered his care to Steve and reached out to Steve's family, anticipating the care he would continue to offer them after Steve's death. These gifted individuals represented a fuller team of social workers, other physicians, music therapists and volunteers, who regularly reviewed Steve's and his family's needs and questions. Steve wrote in his blog:

This new team will walk me to the finish line of this life. I will have whatever medical, social, and spiritual support I need from both the hospice team and our family, friends, church and seminary families.

And later:

Today, I'm relaxing into gratitude for having such good care. Today, I'm not afraid, though some fears will undoubtedly sneak up on me as I get sicker. Today, I'm trying to be attentive to what is happening to me without feeling that I have to be responsible for everything. Today, I am living once again into joy.

For me, as a physician, to be a part of this team approach of hospice care continued to offer an enormous freedom and comfort, a style of collaborative and collegial medical practice I had missed in my clinic career, and another welcomed transition in my life.

Another transition for Steve and his family, and for all hospice patients, is the changes in relationships in their lives. Just a matter of days after our first meeting, I was asked to join Steve and Sharol again, this time with Tim Dearborn, a close friend from Steve's young adulthood, who is now a fellow pastor and theologian. In the few days they spent together at the end of Steve's life, this friend and colleague became a pastor as well to Steve and Sharol. Freed and empowered by their shared faith and their long-term friendship, Tim led the four of us in probing tough questions: what would Steve's last days be like? What could he expect to be able to do. . . and not do? How did I think they should or could plan for the time he had left? How would he and his family, and we in hospice, deal with his worsening symptoms?

The conversation marked a notable change in my relationship with Steve and Sharol, and initiated a relationship with Tim, as I transitioned from being merely their physician to becoming their friend and fellow disciple on this journey of faith we all share. My answer to Tim's question about how they should spend their remaining time was to do what they expect to do for all eternity together, in an intentional way. I said I didn't know what that would be for them, though I suspected it might be some experience of worship, since they are both preachers and gifted musicians.

I explained that for Bill and me, it had been the Sacrament of the Eucharist. I am not sure what I think about heaven, about where Bill is or even if Bill is between now and the Resurrection, except that whenever I come to the Lord's Table, I know with the certainty of faith that he is already at that Feast (probably teaching little cherubs to play with their food!). In retrospect, that conviction, that knowledge transformed my memories of all the Communions in which our pastor had led us as Bill was dying: they have become the first tastes of our transformed marriage, of our always-deepening, ever-healing relationship.

I did not know, but Tim did, that Steve and Sharol were "high Sacramentalists" long before I was. Sharol wrote me that afternoon that Tim had led them in a Communion service before he left to return to his home. A couple of days later, she invited me to share that example during Steve's last Communion before his death, celebrated with his family and seminary colleagues in their bedroom, celebrated with great joy, deep faith, and poignant tenderness. Knowing that I shared something beyond symptom control with them, something that might shape their future in a lasting way, moved me deeply. As I had learned with Lucy, the "healthy boundaries" of established roles are sometimes barriers to love and friendship, barriers which the Spirit of the One Who calls us "Friends" insists on transcending and transforming.

After we finished talking, the four of us wept together, as Steve and Sharol parted with dreams and entrusted God with one another's care. None of us anticipated that in a mere thirty-six hours, Steve would begin actively dying.

The intense and unexpected community that forms in the face of death is another extraordinary transition. Steve's family, neighbors and friends gathered to begin keeping a vigil around his bed, in his home and across the street at the seminary which loved him so. The vigil rapidly spread across the country to include other family members, his former students, close friends, and even acquaintances the Hayners had never met but had come to know through their blogging. Together, we were awestruck by the power of such bonds to transcend time and distance. During the following four days, those of us who gathered reflected with Steve, Sharol and their children, on the power of shared faith, and how the language and experiences of faith enabled us to love one another so quickly and so deeply. We marveled at the details and resiliency of the human body as Steve continued to live and converse, and even e-mail and text his good-byes. We were comforted and assured by the community of discernment we became, helping each of us hear God-sent calls, and respond to urges to come to their home and to care for one another.

Later one of his friends sent me a photograph he had made, of three families sitting on the steps to Steve's room during the last hour of his life. An older couple at the top of the stairs, their gazes locked and hands held, contemplated their own separation by death. Beneath them, two beautiful, sensitive, faith-full sisters, teenagers at the very edge of adulthood are beginning that transition in earnest as they comfort their pained parents, whose arms are uplifted in prayer. At the bottom of the steps is a younger couple, their children playing in the room below, not yet even on the stairs, not yet aware of the transitions death will one day force upon them.

Set apart from the family by the architecture of their home, but gathered with them in the extraordinary power of God's Spirit, and connected by modern technology to friends and family scattered across the continent, they prayed and sang hymns with his family. As the moment of his death approached and joy filled the room, their tearful unison singing became harmony and descants. Moments like that make it clear why ancient Celtic Christians described death as the fleeting moments when heaven and earth meet. To be present at those moments, to become a part of those communities, to answer an awesome call to be a vehicle to contribute to that healing – those are the great blessings of being a hospice caregiver.

Postscript: Another Transition

Shortly before this chapter was due to the editors of this book, I had a routine follow-up appointment with the nurse practitioner in interventional cardiology. When she asked, I told her I had had no pain since my stents eleven months earlier, and I had increased my daily workout on the treadmill in length, speed and incline. At that point, I felt some chest pressure, but never pain; I wasn't too concerned about it, but thought she should know. She immediately scheduled a stress test for later that afternoon. The stress test was positive, and the next afternoon I returned to the catheterization lab for additional stents.

I had known there was about a thirty percent chance of a bare metal stent restenosing, and that the only way to control my coronary disease would be radical life- style changes. I had made all those changes: weight loss, exercise, cholesterol reduction, stress management, job change. In spite of it all, my disease had progressed; now less serious lesions on last year's studies have worsened.

Now I share the emotional and spiritual turmoil of my hospice patients. I am not yet in hospice care as it is legally defined, but philosophically – and emotionally – that is the transition in which I am engaged. My demon has been named, but was not exorcised. I now know I will probably die of heart disease, but not how or when. That moment could come suddenly with an arrhythmia, and my active dying will be blessedly brief but very lonely; or I may die a prolonged and uncomfortable death with congestive heart failure, but surrounded again in prayer and song. Time seems so much more precious, but I am wont to spend it pondering which type of death I would prefer, as if I have some choice.

Living with death, living "in hospice" means living, intentionally, purposefully, hopefully. Tears come easily, but also joyfully; new friendships delight and old friendships sustain. Living with death means learning what matters in my life, and pursuing those things. It means nurturing relationships. It means praying joyfully, and praying with others who are facing down their own deaths. It means coming to the Lord's Table to experience the companionship of all the Saints, and to taste the feast for which I yearn. It means grieving for the future I will not have, and therefore celebrating at every opportunity. Above all, it means a life of gratitude for the gifts of God's Spirit: family, community, church and creation.

Order: Joy in the Journey by Steve and Sharol Hayner. Copyright (c) 2015 by Steve and Sharol Hayner. InterVarsity Press: Downers Grove, IL, USA.

PART III

REFLECTIONS ON TRANSITIONS

Suggestions to Persons in Transition

For a couple of years I had thought about hosting a retreat for a group of men and women whom I had met in travels back and forth across the country. All of these were bright, energetic and committed disciples. All but three were ordained ministers. After determining that I should bring these persons together, I asked a friend of mine if he would be interested in funding the first gathering.

When he agreed to pick up the tab for a week at the Monastery of the Holy Spirit in Conyers, Georgia, I assembled the list and sent the invitations. There were twenty of us who gathered for a week of prayer, sharing and silence all mixed into a refreshing, liberating time together.

I had some resistance to labeling myself a mentor to these intelligent and creative ministers and three laypersons making up the group. As a consequence I had a rather laid back posture toward the group and though the meeting times were announced, the content of those times together flowed with the spirit of the gathering.

During the late afternoon of the last night that we were together, I had an inspiration to speak to the group. Heretofore, I had offered guided reflections, aided with Lectio Divina, and had spoken privately to everyone present. But this afternoon I felt a strong urge to share with the group some of the things that I had learned about living during my seven decades. I took a sheet of scrap paper and began to jot down a few notes from which I intended to speak. The statements that I made that evening were in the form of admonitions – like what a professor might say to his students or a parent might speak to a child or, perhaps, like an old man speaking to persons he had mentored for a number of years. Most of these admonitions were followed with testimony of how I had come to that insight or why I thought it to be important for life. Here are those nine admonitions.

1.
Accept the self that God created.

In the end there is no other choice. You are who you are with the gifts and possibilities that have been given to you. You may wish that you were more beautiful or handsome, that you had greater gifts or greater opportunities. But your life is what it is. You are where you are! In the future it may change or you may change, but for the moment you are in this particular situation.

The acceptance of my own selfhood has been a lifelong battle for me. I have wanted to be other than the "I" that God made me. I looked at others and yearned to be like them. They could do important things in ways that I could not. They had gifts that dwarfed my own. Too often I envied others when they received acclaim. Something must be wrong with me. My "self" was not good enough or talented enough.

This war with self-acceptance was perhaps a battle with insecurity and inferiority. As I have battled this handicap, I have uncovered a habit that contributed to my unhappiness. I discovered that in nearly every instance of envy or jealousy of a fellow human being, I compared his or her strongest points with my weaker ones. Seldom did I identify my strength as comparable with his or hers. This habit of false comparison set the stage for me to keep alive my feelings of inadequacy.

Finally came the day that I decided, "I am a human being" and there is not another exactly like me. I have gifts and potentiality that no one else possesses in the same manner and to the same degree. I am what I am, and that is good enough for God and it is good enough for me.

So, I admonish you to accept the person you are. Discover this person and become fully the individual that you were created to be.

2.
Live in the rhythm of your life.

Life is like a stream of water. Sometimes it flows fast, at other times slow, and sometimes it eddies. If the stream is fast and you are unprepared, it's dangerous; if it is slow and you are pushing the stream, you get worn out; if it eddies and you are impatient, you get discouraged. Live in the flow of your life.

My issue has been seeking to live beyond myself. When I became a follower of Christ at age seventeen, my mentors were all forty or fifty years old. They gave me cues for my life of faith. The books I read as a young Christian revealed the commitment and perseverance of the saints. I had an ideal picture of what it meant to follow Jesus, and I was determined, with a fair degree of ego expansion, to be the best disciple he ever had.

As a consequence of this ideal and commitment, I looked for the same maturity at twenty that came when I was fifty, and I developed further in the next two decades. In every stage of life I seemed always to be striving to live in the next stage or beyond it. By taking this approach to life, I was never content to be where I was. I was never happy with my progress because my goal was just out of reach, just beyond me.

The pace of life changes. Like rivers, our lives rush at times and at other times slow to a trickle. I seem to have lived much of my life with only two speeds: full throttle or dead stopped. I have wasted too much energy resisting the current rather than relaxing into its flow.

Stages of life are for learning and experiencing the fullness present at each level of maturity. When we refuse to stay in the flow, we begin to wish we were someone else, doing something else in some other place.

Be where you are.

Live in the stage you are in.

Don't try to be seventy or eighty when you are twenty or thirty!

3.
Dare to take risks.

Each person has his or her own particular capacity for risk, so there's no need to be heroic. Don't risk just to be risking. Risk when you are called. Risk when new doors open. Risk when challenges come knocking on your door.

For many of us failure reveals a deep flaw in our character or, at least, others' estimate of us. I have taken many risks, but I would like to tell you of one that paid rich dividends. When I left Phenix City, Alabama to study for the Ph.D. at Emory, I had no house to move into, no money to pay tuition, and no salary to support a family. I had nothing to lose, so if I lost everything, I would only be even.

I earnestly prayed all night before making this move. That night around the altar of the church Abraham became my patron saint. He was called. He obeyed. And he went out "not knowing." I discovered that night that risk is taking the way of "unknowing."

This risk changed my whole life forever. In wonderful ways all our needs for food, shelter and income were met. I had a strange kind of happiness, simply depending upon God for my livelihood.

In Atlanta my ship's sails were hoisted and the winds blew in new directions. Doors opened that I never dreamed of. My efforts in ministry were rewarded , and the course of my life changed. This move from Phenix City to Atlanta altered my life dramatically.

4.
Embrace your failures.

Your failures, when denied, become the accusers of your soul; your failures accepted can become your greatest strength. If you give failures too much power, they will paralyze your actions. You will do nothing for fear of failure. This fear is fueled by the notion that others will mock your efforts or that your superego will become a ruthless accuser.

No act is a failure if you learn from it. Do you think that we come into this world with a sufficient knowledge of life? Can we live mistake-free lives? How do we ever learn if we do not risk failure?

I have numerous experiences in my life that could be dubbed "failures." I have created several programs for congregations that soured on the shelf for lack of interest or effectiveness. But on the other hand I have created a dozen programs that touched the lives of thousands of persons over the space of thirty-plus years.

I have failed in relationships. Having to terminate a friend's employment usually ruptures the relationship. Unconscious acts and misunderstood motives have cooled other relations. Divorce is public for all to see. When I was in the midst of my divorce, I thought that everyone I met already knew about it, as if it had been headline news. Furthermore, since I was a Christian and a minister with a public persona, I felt that I owed everyone an explanation of why the marriage failed.

In this hypersensitivity I discovered an astounding fact. Most people did not care about me, my failure and my self-pity. They were focused on themselves and gave little thought to my pain, embarrassment and guilt.

You care far more about your failures than do others!

Yet, in this failure I learned that I was capable of any sin committed by anyone else. The awareness of my vulnerability knocked off the pious, self-righteous dressing of my soul. As never before, I had a compassionate sensitivity for persons who have failed in their high intentions.

I hope that you will not let your failure, any failure, paralyze you. Own it, admit it and move on with your life.

5.
Attend the Voice of the Spirit within.

The Spirit speaks to us in both small and large ways. Listen to that inner voice deep within you. Of course, we must always discern whether it is God or us or God in us, but the discernment is not as difficult as many imagine. After years of listening, you will find that following the Spirit becomes a practiced way of life.

The major decisions in my life have come in response to the Voice of God. Before I went to Columbia Theological Seminary as a professor, the Voice spoke to me on New Year's Day of 1978. I was asking what I should do with my life that year when a flood of images and ideas came into my mind.

Among these words were, "Finish your Ph.D. dissertation because one day you may wish to teach." To complicate the act of obedience, you should know that I began work on the degree in 1963, and now I was being directed to apply for an extension fifteen years later. Any academic dean or member of a graduate school committee would tell you that it was impossible. But there were extenuating circumstances.

I telephoned my major professor with whom I had worked for four years before throwing in the towel. When he answered the phone, I queried, "Is there a possibility that I could resurrect my Ph.D. program?" He responded, "I don't see why not; a few days ago Dean Lester noted that we are in the business of giving degrees and not withholding them."

After fifteen years my program received a resurrection, and the dissertation that I could not write in four years, I wrote in six months.

I believe in the accuracy of the Inner Voice. Had I not listened to this guidance, the next twenty years of my life would have been very, very different.

6.
Cultivate hope.

In the darkest hour look for the glimmer of light. The light does shine in the darkness if we can perceive it. Hope gives joy and meaning to the present. Hope provides energy and drive.

I think of hope as a positive or acceptable image of the future. This acceptable future can be anything from a happy marriage to the education of a child to finding a worthy vocation. Whatever that image of the future may be, it gives a reason for living in the present. When we cannot imagine a positive future, we are in trouble. Having no future means that no purpose exists in our life, and the anxiety of having no future overly burdens the present.

Those of us who have experienced deep grief or remorse know how either of these wipes out the future. For example, I have visited women whose husband had recently died. Many of these women have said, "I cannot imagine my life without him." And, that is true; they cannot imagine their lives as being different from what they had expected.

When the future is dark, gloomy or fearful, wait. Wait for the clouds to clear and the darkness to break up. You cannot deceive your soul by pretending with positive thinking and mind manipulation that you have an alluring future. The birth of hope comes from within as we continue seeking to hear God through the mist and the pain. Generally, hope comes in little flashes, and the future begins to take form slowly. You cannot rush this process.

Michelle Voss shared these words with me:

"You need not leave your room,

Remain sitting at your table and listen.

You need not even listen, simply wait.

You need not even wait; just learn to become quiet and still and solitary.

The world will freely offer itself to you to be unmasked. It has no choice; it will roll in ecstasy at your feet." (Franz Kafka)

One period of lost hope for me came soon after Nan and I were married. I had been in a long, dry, stale period. I knew that vocationally I was not where God intended, but I had no idea what God's intention was. Sometimes we know what we will not being doing long before we learn what we will be doing. During this time I went on a three-day silent retreat to listen for God. I thought that surely God would reveal to me the future direction of my life.

During the three days I prayed, read scripture and listened. No words. No fresh intuition. On the last day as I knelt to pray, nine skinny little words flowed through my mind: *"You are a servant of the Lord in waiting."* I waited. I had no choice and the way opened before me.

Psalm 16:11 seems apropos: "You show me the path of life. In your presence there is fullness of joy; in your right hand are pleasures forevermore."

7.
Live in the present.

This prayer from *Living before God* sets the stage for this admonition:

LIVING BEFORE GOD

Gracious God,
We are before you,
We are always before you.

You see us as we are and
Love us for ourselves.
You hear the words
We cannot say,
You know the longing
We cannot express.

Grant that it be enough for us
To be seen,
To be known, and
To be loved by you this moment.

AMEN

Live in the present moment because in this moment the infinity of the mystery of God is being manifest. This moment bears the presence of God and the joy that overflows from it. The present moment is a sacrament, according to Jean Pierre de Caussade. As a sacrament, time is the natural aspect of the moment, and the infusion of the divine presence is the holy aspect of the moment. The moment mediates both; it is our task to ingest what the moment brings. The present moment opens the door to the Transcendent as it manifests the infinity of the mystery of God. It invites contemplation.

The temptation for us all resides in the attraction of the past with its known ways or the lure of the future with its possibilities, but to give our attention either to the past or to the future takes us away from the present moment. If the present moment is the meaning of holiness, as a professor friend of mine likes to say, what is there to gain by leaving it? If the present is the place of God, learn ways to abide there and listen for the guidance of the One who is always coming to you.

Throughout the day you can repeatedly admonish yourself: "Come to the present." These words can become a habit or a mantra that reminds you of some very important things. Though I have not mastered a life continuously centered in the present, it is my deep desire and my enduring goal. Hear this admonition:

Come to the present. It is
　　…. the time that you have
　　…. the place of your life
　　….the place of God's grace.
Come to the present. It is
　　….all that you have
　　….where all obedience begins.
Come to the present:
The Place of God.

8.
Keep editing your story.

You have been constructing your story since before you remember. You have told it to yourself a thousand times and you keep telling it. If you keep listening to the story you are telling yourself, you will likely have new insights and persuasions that will change it. New perspectives give us better vision or, at least, different points of sighting. One of the tasks of life is to get your story straight. If "the fruit of the future is in the roots of the past," you may get some interesting and helpful clues by digging around the roots of your life.

One of the drivers in everyone's story is the stage of life in which we are living. Youth, middle age, old age – each time we pass through a state of awareness, the world is different for us.

Editing your story will benefit you in a number of ways. When you review things long past that originally seemed detrimental to your life, you may discover that your responses to the pain or failure actually made you a better person.

When you edit your story, you will also discover themes that have run through your whole life. These themes not only give your life cohesion, but they suggest your gifts and what your life has been about and likely the directions it will take in the future.

During most of my early life I felt inferior. When I revisit those experiences that gave me feelings of inferiority, I discover that I misinterpreted them. For example, I was reared in the rural South, and some people spoke disparagingly about my origin. I recall visits to my cousins in the county seat town nearby and being introduced as "the country cousin." The secondhand clothes that I wore did not lift my self-esteem either.

Yet, in my adult years when I revisit these memories, I can edit my responses to these statements, which probably had no discounting quality in them. I can tell myself that being a country boy does not make me inferior, and wearing hand-me-down clothes does not affect my personal worth. When I accept my origin as a poor kid, I can be grateful for the kindness shown me and get on with my life.

Keep editing your story because "it ain't over until it's over," as Yogi would say.

9.
Do not be afraid of death.

Nearly all my life I feared death. Sometimes fear kept me awake at night and at other times it invaded my day with its disturbing face. When I was a child, I put off thinking about it because I thought only old people died; in my adolescence, I was tormented with the brevity of life; even when I reached middle age, I still was pressed by the reality of death.

At age fifty for the first time it occurred to me that it would not be so tragic to die. I could rest from my anxiety. Then an amazing thing happened, and I do not know how it occurred.

Somewhere between the ages of sixty-three and sixty-eight one day I awoke to an amazing gift: the fear of death had disappeared from my consciousness. I could honestly say, "I am no longer afraid of death."

Wrapped up in this fear was also the incomprehensibility of eternity – forever and ever and ever. On occasion I am still shattered by this reality. One day I wondered if God ever felt what eternity was like. And, I wondered if God created the world and all that is within it because God's Eternal Being needed something to do and someone to love.

Today, I often find myself looking with expectancy to the next stage of the journey. What will it be like? How will all our earthly schooling in life affect us when the path moves on? I want to be awake and alert when I make this transition. On two occasions I have discussed with my doctor that I do not want to be filled with opiates on the eve of my death. I have struggled with the issue too long not to be aware of it. I pray for a good death.

Living the Questions of Life's Transitions

Life moves in a series of transitions, and every transition offers an invitation for transformation. Without argument, living through transitions requires energy and attention, and transitions inevitably move us toward growth or decay, new life or death. Can we accept transitions, even difficult or painful ones, as a pathway to transformative growth?

We were all born and passed from the womb of darkness to the world of light – a transition. We all pass from this world into the Great Silence at the end – a transition. Between these two major transitions we journey through life and experience a plethora of adaptations, adjustments and alterations like. . .

- Losing our first teeth and growing new ones.
- Leaving home for school.
- Moving from one grade to the next one.
- Choosing a mate.
- Getting a job.
- Engaging in relationships with others.
- Birthing and caring for children.
- Growing old and losing some of our power.

Those are such common transitions that we more or less expect them, but there are others that take us by surprise:

- An incurable illness.
- The loss of a job.
- A divorce
- The death of a child.
- The untimely death of a parent.
- Bankruptcy
- A fatal accident
- Betrayal by a friend.
- Unfaithful spouse

Changes Come to All

Whether anticipated or not, transitions change us; they change the way we see and live in the world, and they make changes inside of us. Take, for example, a six-year-old who leaves home for his first day at school. This occurrence changes his place in the world. No longer is mother available at his beck and call; no longer is he free to get up and wander around the room as he did the day before. His external world has changed, and his sense of well-being will depend upon his internal adjustment. These simple principles to a large extent describe all of the anticipated transitions in life. But the unexpected transitions are different. The person experiencing a transition through an unanticipated event has no power to prevent the occurrence. The person surprised by tragedy has only one choice – how will I respond to this unexpected interruption in my life?

The teenage daughter is driving home from school when another driver runs the red light, smashes into her car and the young person is left paralyzed for the remainder of her life. How will she respond to the incident? How will her parents respond?

A man at the apex of his career who should have another twenty years of service goes for an annual checkup. His blood test has some abnormal cells present. After additional testing and an MRI, he receives the news that he has pancreatic cancer – six months to live. He cannot stand up to this alien that has invaded his body! Even with all the different therapies, he can only decide how he will respond.

A woman whose job demands travel returns early from a business trip. She makes her way home and when she enters the house, she discovers her husband in bed with another woman. Unplanned. Unexpected. Unanticipated but real and tragic. In this and a myriad of other difficult examples, there is no way to see what's coming or prepare for the inevitable changes. The disappointment or the pain that results may at first be experienced as a subtle ache or a dulling numbness. Whether the initial feelings are intense or not, when reality sets in, a decision or response must be made that will inform a new way of being in the world.

A person who enters a transition is never the same person who emerges from it. Whether or not the transition is acknowledged, accepted, expected, surprising, gradual, or abrupt, it makes no difference. Change always occurs. These changes may be creative or destructive; they may be transformative or tragic. Consider a young woman enrolling in college to prepare herself to be a teacher. She studies hard, completes her course requirements and seeks a job. In this series of events she experiences at least three transitions: she transitions from home to college, from friends in high school to friends in college, and she experiences independence in getting a job and earning her own living. These transitions can be anticipated, prepared for, and intentional. For this student these transitions, successfully negotiated, result in a transformation of how she sees herself, how she connects to the world and how she matures.

By contrast, consider the parents of a child who suffered an untimely death. First, there was no way to prepare for this event. It came unexpectedly with devastating blows. Shock and deep grief accompany this catastrophe. The parents have to reconsider who they are, how they see the world and how they will navigate the pain and the changes that have invaded their lives. There are several possible responses: why did this happen to us? How can we believe in a good God who let this happen? Where did we fail? These are questions that never will be answered to their satisfaction. If they continue asking these questions and never get beyond them, it would be a tragedy.

On the other hand, when they are able to face the harsh yet undeniable reality that their child is dead and will not return to this life, that they cannot change this tragedy, that they can only change their response to life as it is, it is much more likely that they will experience transformation. Our strong intention in writing this book and telling stories of positive transformation is to provide our readers a new way of seeing their own lives and making the kinds of choices that lead to transformation.

What Shapes Our Transitions?

We believe there are at least four drivers in this quest for a fulfilled life: 1) basic survival needs, 2) cultural expectations including role models, 3) the quest for meaning, and 4) hope for an acceptable future. These dimensions of human need coalesce to influence nearly all of our decisions. Perhaps the examination of a particular transition will illustrate how these drivers work in shaping a life. Consider a young adult who finishes college and is looking for the right job.

Why would a college graduate feel the need of a career? First of all, his parents have informed him that one day he must make his own living, find his own house and secure his future. This makes sense to him because he has had food, clothing and shelter in his parents' home. His father has been a role model for getting a job, making a living and taking care of his family. When he looks beyond his family, he recognizes that other men whom he respects are engaged in the same tasks. Furthermore, the larger culture in which he has been reared places this expectation upon every young man. When he finishes college and enters into the workaday world, he then begins to consider job security, salary and how he can adequately prepare for the future. Obviously, his individual needs, the cultural demands made on him and the vocation that he has chosen, all combine to shape his life. Disruption in any one of these areas creates a potential crisis. For example, he gets laid off from his job or his father dies; his seemingly smooth life now becomes chaotic. These drivers in his life, the transitions that come with his vocation, whether pertaining to preparation, a promotion or the loss of a job, precipitate serious transitions.

The issue of meaning lies at the heart of this quest for fulfillment and stability. The questions of being and meaning persist throughout a lifetime. How do I live life fully and well? What brings meaning, purpose, joy, and vitality to life? What is life asking of me now? Not one of these soul-deep questions is ever finally answered, but throughout life, growing and transformative people continue to live into these questions and perhaps breathe into answers, again and again.

Asking the questions

We believe that asking and seeking answers to foundational questions of life can initiate a transition that results in transformation. Whether these questions spring from a natural quest or are precipitated by unexpected events, they will be asked either consciously or unconsciously. These questions are as old as life, yet we ask them over and over again until we arrive at a clearer understanding. Simply being human gives birth to questions. Consider these most basic questions and ponder the place where these questions are born:

Where did I come from?

Who am I?

What am I doing here?

Where will I go after this life?

While they may seem simple on the surface, in a peculiar way the answers to these questions keep changing. The questions in all their naked simplicity persist in ways that force us to keep probing the deeper levels of awareness. Like a miner digging for gold, our incessant restlessness keeps us clawing for deeper and deeper insights that help us realize what it means to be a human being.

The persistent question of meaning takes priority over all other questions. If men and women can find a "why to live," they can find a "how to live." If only we took time in our busy lives to reflect, we likely would find a yearning for something more than we have yet realized. Most people sense an ache or a restlessness for something in life, even if it is not obvious. They have a yearning for something more, a desire to find the hidden treasure, but they do not know how to define this quest, nor do they know how to begin it. This quest seems to be part of the spiritual DNA of the human condition.

Why would a person who in no way considers herself to be religious, nevertheless say that an event was meant to be? If it is meant to be, who meant it to be? Yet people seek answers. Why?

Other seekers may have had childhood experiences grounded in a religious tradition, yet no longer feel it necessary or essential for their lives. At a somewhat predictable stage in life these persons begin to question the validity of the beliefs and values professed in religious institutions, no matter the faith tradition. Their questions often arise as they observe what seems to be the hypocrisy of those who profess faith and yet have avoided the deep unanswered questions with which they live.

All faiths have constituents who have been reared in their particular religious culture and have absorbed the beliefs of that culture, but they no longer find the traditional answers satisfying. Do you recognize how a short-sighted answer to the fundamental questions of life can go unanswered?

Where to begin

Begin pondering the questions. Persons who engage in a serious quest for what is genuine and real often ask these Who? What? Why? or Where? questions. They press for answers because something in their depths drives them to seek. For example, the answer to the seminal question of "Who am I" includes more than a psychological profile.

The question about purpose, "Why am I here," also has deeper levels of understanding. I am here to breathe the air and drink the water. I am here to reproduce children. I am here to work and accomplish goals. Am I also here to discover the meaning of life, the meaning of my one and only life? Am I here to be in relationship and harmony with all of creation? Am I and all the other people here commissioned to complete the creation? As the poet Mary Oliver asks, "What will you do with your one wild and precious life?"

The "where" question points toward the future; it is directional in nature. Where am I going in my life, in my family and in my vocation? Ultimately, where am I going? Is there something beyond life on earth as we know it? Is there another dimension of being from which we have come, and to which we are returning?

Open, honest questions awaken something deep within us, and merely asking them invites a powerful drive to engage the unexplored dimensions of our lives. Once we have begun to ask these questions with existential seriousness, life becomes one long pursuit of meaning and fulfillment – one transition after another. Each of us is a researcher, searching again and again, and our life is a living laboratory for discovering and appropriating the compelling and transformative answers that we find.

In setting forth the existential questions, we have given you a way to think about engaging in your own transformation. Finding the words to express the nature and meaning of transitions presents another set of challenges: what words do we use? How can we recognize the presence of a transition? What are the decisions that lead to transformation? As we have lived these questions, we have found that metaphors and images help us discover and communicate insights into life transitions. We use metaphors because they are less precise, amorphous, suggestive and have the capability of conveying the complexities in life. They open us to the possibility and promise of paradox and allow us to live in the gap of the way things are and the way we yearn for them to be. For example, a flowing stream, a chambered nautilus, and the birth metaphor emerged in our conversations as useful in seeing the possibilities for transformation through transition.

Metaphors to Invite Meaning in Transition

In our reflections on transition, three metaphors emerged that illustrate various aspects and mysteries of life's transitions: the birth of a baby, the flowing of a stream, and the life of a chambered nautilus. While these metaphors don't illuminate every aspect of transition, each contributes to a fuller understanding of the changes through which we pass. In a sense, they symbolize the ways in which transitions might invite us to live life whole as we seek to make meaning of the dynamic, ever-changing messes and marvels of life.

The Birth Metaphor

Transition is itself a metaphor for birth and change that aims to assimilate the ongoingness of life. We have found that the miraculous and life-changing flow of conception, gestation and birth provides one way of seeing and living through life's natural, yet often jarring transitions. In one sense, the birth of a baby is but one of the many birth experiences that life offers. If this claim sounds odd or strange, perhaps a glimpse into one of our stories will make it clearer.

Imagine a young couple who marry and within a year are surprised to learn they are expecting a baby. After adjusting to the news, they laugh and say, "We know what causes that! Why are we so surprised?" While they do know what causes it on one hand, they really only know of the conditions and actions that make this miracle possible. So they turn to wonder . . . Why us? Why now? Then they wait. On the much anticipated day of the baby's birth the proud father parades through the hospital shouting aloud, "It's a boy! It's a boy!" He distributes traditional cigars to all his friends, as the mother, exhausted from labor and delivery, heaves a sigh of relief and gratitude. Birth was a joyous event. And for the baby, the physical birth was the first of many *births* or transitions in life. And for the parents, the birth of a new life means a new family is born. Life is forever changed.

Fast forward and this same baby boy is now a high school senior.

He begins to feel exhausted playing the sports that once seemed almost effortless. The parents are worried. After many doctor visits, this family, once filled with nothing but joy and hope, is suddenly confronted with the unthinkable news of a rare and life-threatening blood disorder. Frightening and uncertain treatments are discussed, and both the young man and his parents struggle to make sense of what is happening to them. What good can be born of this painful transition? Is it possible that this tragedy might be transformed into a vocational calling and a new life that is now a source of hope and healing for others who are in the midst of life-threatening illnesses?

Through the narrative of various transformations one can begin to see how each is a new birth, a new beginning. Illness marked a new beginning; a birth of sorts, and each experience leaves the young man with a larger sense of meaning. Life experience deposited a greater openness and a larger view of healing for him. Through the many transitions from life-limiting illness to healing professional, there was struggle with confusion, darkness, and pain, along with the encouragement of acceptance, compassion, and hope.

Can you begin to see why we view birth as a good metaphor for the transitions of life? Consider other aspects of the birth metaphor. Conception takes place in darkness and mystery. And just as there is no rational way to explain why a particular sperm fertilizes a certain egg, there is no rational way to explain why a vibrant young teenager suddenly faces the darkness of illness and the threat of life cut way too short. And it is impossible to rationalize a transformation born of the beautiful miracle of new life seeded by the painful transition of unexpected illness. The mystery that lies behind life pervades the birth of a new life. Has it ever struck you what a mystery it is to be human, just the simple feeling of being?

When you recognize that you had nothing to do with your birth, you did not ask for it, you did not earn it; it was given to you. And no response is more appropriate than gratitude. Whatever inexplicable miracle brought us into being, has the marks of generosity and love.

The birth metaphor also suggests an internal guidance system and the possibility found in life's unfolding miracles. Letting go of control and constant striving allows a space to listen deeply so that inner wisdom may simply emerge. For example, how does the fertilized egg know to detach itself and glide down the fallopian tube and attach itself to the wall of the uterus? The direction of life develops with one organ after the other. Does this not suggest that there is something within our human nature that knows just how it wants to grow. Consider the lilies of the field; they don't toil or spin! All humans, men and women alike, have this internal guidance system. It is possible to live life as an unfolding mystery to be experienced rather than a problem to be solved! Whether in expected or unexpected transitions, when we listen within, can we not hear a still small voice guiding us to transform pain into possibility? The pain of birth, again and again, offers hope of new life.

The Stream Metaphor

Life is like a flowing stream! The stream did not ask to be; it began as a pool of water in the earth, a rain cloud in the sky or melted snow off the mountain. The stream is guided by a force outside itself; it is drawn downhill until it merges with the great ocean. As a broad river, it is deep and then shallow; it is now clear and then muddy; it often flows rapidly and sometimes lazily; it rushes like a runner in a marathon and rests like a cat in the sun. When the stream is a broad river, it carries heavy loads of commerce; when the stream is a sparkling brook, it dances and sings. When the stream is clear and still, it reflects the beauty that surrounds it. Does this give a hint of what happens when we are living in the flow of our lives?

What would it be like to float on your back in a moving stream watching the trees pass by, and staring at the blue sky?

What would it be like to get stuck in an activity and go around and around and around like a leaf restrained in an eddy?

What would it be like to dive into a clear river, swim to the bottom and look at its depth?

What would it be like to glide downstream in a canoe and pass under a large limb? How would it feel to grasp the limb and experience the tug of the river against your canoe?

Can we hear the song that arises from the impeded stream, or are we so fixated on the rock that blocks the rush of the water that we miss the song? How is life like a river, a flowing stream, for you?

The Chambered Nautilus

Perhaps this creature is unknown to you. This curious-looking inhabitant of the sea has remained unchanged for over 400 million years. Though oddly shaped, it can attain speeds of over two knots. A small tube near the animal's tentacles expels water under pressure that propels the nautilus.

The curious thing about the nautilus is the shell containing many individual chambers. Each chamber is individually sealed, and the creature regulates the density of the chamber by injecting or removing fluid. When a young nautilus begins its life, it begins with seven chambers. As it grows, it adds new chambers to its shell, each a little larger than the previous one.

The chambered nautilus can be a useful image for the various transitions through the developmental stages of life. This amazing creature carries its history on its back just as we do. Each chamber in the shell represents a place the nautilus once lived. These chambers at one time were large enough to provide shelter and protection for the nautilus but as the creature grew, it required larger and larger chambers. Though it does not continue to live in the early chambers, each chamber remains critical for the nautilus throughout life; it provides a source of important life lessons. Space that was adequate at one stage of life becomes too small and limiting for the next stage. Life always moves forward into ever-expanding spaces, or it falls back into a limited existence. For the nautilus, life is a process of continually moving into larger and more inclusive spaces. Is this process possible for us? Can the nautilus teach us about a transformation that provides space for all of life's experience, allowing us to carry on our lives without our past becoming too heavy?

Accepting Life's Invitations to Wholeness

Ideally, as we move through transitions in life, we are constantly making new choices, gaining fresh insights and expanding our rigid boundaries; this is transformation. Isolation, fear, secretive living and defensiveness derail transformation and keep us stuck in the smaller chambers in life. Can we be at home in each chamber and accept the possibility that every transition is an invitation to wholeness? The stories and lives represented in this book offer evidence that yes, every transition can be an invitation to wholeness. It's a lifelong process of *living the questions* and discovering the infinite possibilities that emerge when we remember to. . .

Accept the self that God created.
Live in the rhythm of your life.
Dare to take risks.
Embrace your failures.
Attend the Voice of the Spirit Within.
Cultivate hope.
Live in the present.
Keep editing your story.
Do not be afraid of death.

ACKNOWLEDGMENTS

Thanks to Our Contributors

We appreciate the contribution that each of the following persons has made to this book. Their stories speak to us all and give us encouragement and hope as we pass through our own transitions.

Robby Carroll
Judy Durff
Hal Edwards
Stacey Hughes
Ben Johnson
Darren Johnson
Jackie Kanfar
Ben Lang
Sanders O'Toole
Richelle Patton
Richard Phillips
Elizabeth Smith-Purcell
Barbara Reeves
Oliva Groover
Betsy Smith
Kay Stewart
Mary Virginia Parrish
Marilyn Washburn
Sarah Wikle
Gareth J. Young

For further exploration into *life's transitions as invitations to wholeness...*

You're invited to write your *story-gatherers and inquiry partners* to learn about retreat and workshop opportunities around this theme. Ben (bjohn1923@aol.com), Robby (robbycarroll@mac.com), and Kay (kay@stillwatersmindfulness.com) will be delighted to share in the unfolding of your life.

A little more about your authors and their work...

Robby Carroll came to ministry as a second career. After graduating from seminary he was ordained a Presbyterian Teaching Elder and he has served on the staffs of three churches and has been in private practice as a Marriage and Family Therapist for thirty-five years. During those years he studied, acquired and practiced a number of counseling skills that included psychoanalyst insights, neurolinguistic programing, eye movement therapy, Marriage and Family Therapy, Guided Imagery, Cognitive Behavioral Therapy and The Enneagram Personality Profile. Both in his life and practice of ministry he has drawn on these and other approaches to achieve healing and wholeness.

In addition to marriage and family counseling, Robby has led support groups like Caregivers for Alzheimers patients, Divorce Recovery and Continuing Care for Alcohol and Drug Recovery. He has trained lay men and women in listening skills for Stephen Ministers. To explore opportunities to work with Robby visit www.robbycarroll.com

Ben Campbell Johnson is Professor Emeritus, Columbia Theological Seminary in Decatur, Georgia. In that setting he taught Evangelism and Church Growth for fifteen years and the last five years he founded the Certificate in Christian Spirituality and taught Christian Spirituality in the seminary curriculum.

Since his retirement from Columbia, he has engaged extensively in interfaith relations, work with refugees and writing biographies with a number of Christian leaders. He and a lifelong friend, Walter Albritton, are assisting people in reflecting, writing, and publishing their personal story. To learn more or to get started with your own writing, go to www.writeyourstorynow.net. Ben believes that writing and reflecting on a life can be extremely helpful in making major transitions.

Kay Stewart facilitates retreats and workshops at the intersection of mindfulness and self-reflective renewal. She currently teaches Mindfulness-based Stress Reduction (MBSR) and other mindfulness-based programs through Shallowford Family Counseling Center in Atlanta.

After 26 years teaching health and fitness at Emory University, Kay completed graduate studies in Mindfulness and Contemplative Education. In 2013, she founded Stillwaters Mindfulness Training to encourage mindful living, joyful connection, and wise action. To learn more about Kay and her inside/out approach to teaching, learning, and living well, go to www.stillwatersmindfulness.com.